HELL OF A CARAVAN PARK

SEPTIMUS COOPER

© Septimus Cooper 2015

All rights reserved.

Septimus cooper has asserted his right under the Copyright, Designs and patents act 1988 to be identified as the author of this book.

No part of this publication may be reproduced, distributed, or transmitted in any form or by any means, without the prior written permission of the author, except in the case of brief quotations embodied in critical reviews and certain other non-commercial uses permitted by copyright law. For permission requests, contact the author.

ISBN-10: 1519355564

ISBN-13: 978-1519355560

Cover design © Socciones

Design & formatting by Socciones Editoria Digitale

www.kindle-publishing-service.co.uk

This book is dedicated to my Mother
Along with many of her profound words of wisdom to me during
my formative years were the following:
"Whatever you be in life be honest and truthful in all your doings."

"The only thing necessary for the triumph of evil is for good men to do nothing."

Edmund Burke
1729-1797

AUTHOR'S BACKGROUND - (A BRIEF RÉSUMÉ)

1940 born Kendal Westmorland (now Cumbria). Raised and lived in Windermere. Attended Windermere Grammar School 1951-1957. Employed by the Borough Treasurer's Department, The Town Hall, Kendal in 1957.

1960 - Joined the Kendal branch of a national industrial banker.

1965 – Moved to Lancashire following promotion to Area Manager, later becoming a self-employed financial consultant.

1985 – Returned home "to avoid the impending rat race" forming a taxi company specialising in scenic tours for the discerning international tourist.

2006 – Septimus retired

INTRODUCTION 1
PREFACE 3
PAUSES FOR THOUGHT 6
1. EARLY WARNING SIGNS 7
2. THE INSURANCE CON 10
3. REPAIRS AND RENEWALS 12
4. A DISGUISED THREAT? 15
5. NAÏVETY? + ENVY? = EGG ON FACE? 17
6. FELL END'S RULES AND REGULATIONS 19
7. HEALTH AND SAFETY 26
INTERLUDE (PAUSE FOR THOUGHT) 29
8. THE "SUPPLY" OF WATER AND ELECTRICITY 30
9. THE ENVIRONMENT 33
10. THE "ON AND OFF ASAP" POLICY? 36
11. REVENUES AND OVERHEADS 38
12. CUSTOMER RELATIONS 44
INTERLUDE – PAUSE FOR THOUGHT 49
13. THE SALES AND BUY-BACKS SECTION I 50
14. A CROWE ON THE PARK 57
15. THE SALES AND BUY-BACKS SECTION II 60
16. NO SALE, NO BUY-BACK 78
17. THE ELECTRICITY FRAUD – PART ONE 80
THE ELECTRICITY FRAUD PART ONE - CONTINUED 87
18. THE EVICTION – AND ITS CONSEQUENCES 113
INTERLUDE – PAUSE FOR THOUGHT 128
19. THE ELECTRICITY FRAUD PART TWO 129

20. FROM DESPAIR TO DELIVERANCE 137
21. ROYLE'S RUINATION 139
22. THE SOLICITORS. THEIR WRITINGS AND THE OUTCOME 153
23. THE REAL ELECTRIC FRAUD – THE COMPLETE TRUTH OF THE MATTER? 188
24. E.O.N. 191
25. OH! THE SUPPLY OF GAS 194
26. CONSCIENCE AND CIVIC DUTY 195
INTERLUDE – PAUSE FOR THOUGHT 202
MISCELLANY 203

INTRODUCTION

Approaching retirement age my wife Margaret and I decided to make the move we had thought about for several years.

Many years ago we spent a great deal of our leisure time holidaying in Scotland, discovering quiet bases where a holiday static caravan was available. This accommodation method was ideal – especially with children – it providing 24/7 freedom (no landlady banging on your door at 8am).

Whilst we were born and bred in the Lake District the caravan scenario was never far from our minds, particularly with what the modern units now had to offer: double glazing, central heating and all the mod cons. All we wanted was the right site for us.

A further persuasive reason for moving was the ever-increasing influx of tourism, together with all its frantic hustle and bustle, especially in the 'honey-pot' area where we lived. Despite this it was a heart-wrenching departure!

Not wishing to stray too far away from our families we decided our 'new lives' would have to be ideally in the Cumbria/North Lancashire area. So, for two years we searched for the site most suitable for our requirements.

Finally, we came across a park which appeared to have everything in our favour, or so it seemed. At the time we might have been, unknowingly, wearing rose-tinted glasses!

We, in our excitement, completely overlooked checking the reputation of the park, the quality of its management, together with any other aspects which could affect our well-being.

However, what finally swayed us into choosing this park was 1. Its geographical location, 2. The nearby estuary, 3. It being near to "an Area of Outstanding Natural Beauty", 4. The plot itself which was set apart from the main site in a woodland clearing, and finally 5. Its proximity to the road and rail network. The Park was called

Fell End.

PREFACE

The book's main intention is to highlight a conspiracy which is based on achieving maximum extraction of holiday home-owners (residents) hard-earned income. This is coupled with an absolute minimum of company expenditure by a certain holiday caravan park, irrespective of how dastardly their actions have to be to implement and achieve their goal. It is obvious that those responsible have been indoctrinated (by who?). They have become immune to the financial and psychological damage they have inflicted on the very people who provide them with a living.

This book is my relatively miniscule attempt to bring certain vile persons of this world to heel. In view of my very limited experience surely whatever I disclose can only be the tip of the termite mound?

The park's actions are life-affecting – no less. It's a trap – an entrapment from the very outset.

It cannot be doubted that there is an excess of wrongdoing in the world, in fact any at all prevents an ideal environment: one which we all yearn for, subconsciously or otherwise. The tragedy is that virtually none of us do anything about it. The reasons for this, I suggest are as follows: -

1. We are wrapped in apathy
2. We prefer 'the quiet life' syndrome
3. We are even prepared to 'turn the other cheek'
4. We lack the academic skills to 'take the fight'
5. We lack clout
6. We lack financial backing to 'take the fight'
7. We are in fear of reprisals by the wrong-doer

One or some or all of these factors prevent us in challenging the evil-doers and their malpractices. If this were not the case what a better world it would be! We look to get away from these annoyances by taking vacations and, although these normally form only part of our lives, they should help our constitutions – like nothing else.

In my case however, the sought-after freedom was not given a chance, as it started to be suffocated from the out-set of my new venture into the world of caravan home-ownership together with the peace and tranquillity I believed it would bring my wife and I at the park we finally chose.

A famous historian once penned the following: -

"The fundamental cause of corruption in the spreading of its web invariably possesses a sharp-fanged spider at its centre"

As you read through this book I hope it is not too much to ask you to subconsciously keep bearing in mind this quotation. It may help in the understanding of, and the fundamental reasons for, the events about to be gradually revealed. In my search for the absolute truth you will notice I sometimes "call a spade a spade". Whilst I may stand accused of lacking in diplomacy, it should help prevent any possible allegations of hypocrisy.

Probably one of the main reasons for the creation of this book is to forewarn others who like me could be plunging into the unknown at tremendous cost to both mind and pocket. Holiday home ownership is fabulous, but beware of the odd despicable, ruthless park. I don't want you to be taught the lesson that I was given. I realise this (my first) book may have its imperfections but consolation comes from the saying 'every book worth reading is imperfect'.

Our experiences which are described in this book are a factual account supported by written evidence (80% estimated). The balance of 20% is supplied by very respectable members of the public, who, if called upon to swear under oath would prove, I'm sure, their genuinity with ease.

In persevering with the progress of the book I believe I have without doubt found it more difficult than the average budding writer. The problems created with my very limited literary prowess are compounded by other factors, namely the following: 1. I may be wrong but when in one's 75th year the mental facilities are not in their prime 2. The lack of any typing or computer skills, or even being able to use the internet etc.. The problem probably lies in the fact that I've become old fashioned and thus (deliberately?) unprogressive. 3. The loss of sight in one eye just prior to my departure from the park. 4. So from a communication point of view I have had to rely solely on the letter and the landline telephone (no mobile). Towards the end of my writings and with the book's publication in sight it became obvious an email facility would be vital. This, therefore, was taken on board and implemented 5. The commencement to completion of my story has all taken place in my leaky, often very cold and sometimes very hot, conservatory. An area 8 foot by 7 foot, together with all the miscellaneous paraphernalia that goes with writing a book. As a schoolboy I was hardened to this type of environment, having to do my homework sat on a wooden seat in the outside backyard lavatory. Further consolation and encouragement I took from the following: - At the time of the book's commencement a recently discovered photograph of my Mother appeared duly framed in my glass study. Somehow I took heart from her daily smile of encouragement.

I might or might not be a believer in fate but I honestly think the bitter experiences I have endured and witnessed at Fell End Park created the springboard of opportunity to write this book.

PAUSES FOR THOUGHT

Whilst creating this book sporadic but inspirational thoughts came unannounced to mind. I felt, however that they weren't directly and strictly relevant to the story; even so I couldn't help jotting them down as an aside. I have kept these thoughts to single figures, "taken the plunge" and included them amongst my writings. Whilst you may not find them as stimulating as I did it is hoped you feel they are worthy of inclusion!

Further inspiration came from the following words pinned up in my office and written by E. Scott Fitzgerald:

"Write for nothing and no one first of all

Write because you must

Write because there is a truth which demands to be burnt onto paper

Write in the face of your lethargy and despair and doubts

Write because you don't know how to write, because you don't know what to believe

But whether defined or abstract, the reader should be someone you love and respect – a person who has the piercing vision to see through any pretence surrounding your work."

1. EARLY WARNING SIGNS

Through the autumn of 2004 we made several visits to Fell End in coming to a deal during which time both parties agreed to our moving onto the park and taking possession on the 1st March 2005. It must be noted that the park's policy was to close down from mid-January to the 28th February.

Mid-November arrived with nothing whatsoever in writing from Fell End. Our requests for same resulted in us receiving, on the 18th November, what their management describes on one of their letter headings "a Statement of Account". We actually requested an invoice together with the terms and conditions of the park. Shown here, you will note there is no date, no V.A.T. and our purchase of one new Willerby Vogue Caravan described as 'Willerby Vouge'. Site fees were also included spelt "sit" and again no V.A.T. present. These fees, £2,440, included the cost of the use of their leisure facilities, namely £400 which we were led to believe were compulsory. At no time were we advised that they were in fact optional. However with an 'in for a penny' carefree attitude we decided to proceed, paid up, and in due course went to view the leisure complex. We were informed initially that it was adjacent to the park, at their company's (pure leisure group ltd.) Watersedge Park. This in truth turned out to be about four miles away. Needless to say we did not use the facility, did not renew same and did not receive a refund.

(R) 18/11/04

FELL END CARAVAN PARK
Slackhead Road. Hale. Nr. Milnthorpe.
Cumbria LA7 7BS.
Tel. 015395 62122 option 2

MR & MRS. S. COOPER
13 ROOMER DRIVE,
WINDEMERE
CUMBRIA
LA23 2LS.

As requested please find statement of account ;

To purchase of Willerby Vouge	£39000-00
Deposit paid	£1000-00
Balance outstanding	£38000-00

Sit fee for 2005 season   £2440-00

If I can be of any further assistance please do not hesitate to give me a call anytime.

Yours sincerely

Avril Proud

(Avril Proudman. Park Manager)

Upon my moving into the area I had the pleasure of meeting a born and bred local gentleman. I later discovered he was very highly respected both for his professionally run business and his sporting skills, thus, to a degree, enhancing the quality of life in the district. I became a faithful customer of his and during our many and inevitable ramblings we touched on Fell End. Some six years ago it came as a great surprise to me when he mentioned that the owner of Fell End Park still owed him from over ten years ago, "about one hundred and twenty pounds from memory" in respect of work done.

2. THE INSURANCE CON

After expressing my ever-increasing disgruntlement to a fellow neighbour, salt was inserted, in all innocence, into my wounded body when he made it quite clear the leisure facilities were definitely an option only.

During the course of our previously mentioned autumnal visits I raised the question of the caravan insurance element. I was assured that all this would be taken care of and indeed in view of the company's "buying power" I would enjoy extremely low discounted rates, way below the norm. In due course, confirmation of cover was received, together with an invoice for £390.00 which we duly paid.

Once again, in conversation with my fellow resident, he advised me to search elsewhere for an insurance quote and at the same time he recommended a national company who specialised in caravan insurance. This company was called Towergate, later to be known as Towergate Bakers. Eventually, and as my first premium was about to lapse, I ignored Pure Leisure's renewal reminders and obtained a quote from Towergate of £245.00 which I duly accepted.

I spread the word as far as I could to my fellow residents, which eventually resulted in everyone receiving a ruling from Pure Leisure that in future all new caravan insurance business must be conducted through the auspices of their office and indeed with an insurance company designated by them. I then discovered to my utter amazement the Pure Leisure Group, all along, were agents of Towergate, no doubt enjoying on top of the sting previously disclosed an introductory commission. As far as I was concerned, they camouflaged their tie-up with Towergate in such a way that the likes of me, a greenhorn to park life, were totally conned. Now you multiply the foregoing by a few thousand units which are under the control of Pure Leisure LTD.'s empire over a caravan's life span of say fifteen years and what do you get? A sinful profit obscene beyond belief. (An example of what is to come?)

I have taken legal advice regarding the structure of their insurance methods and I'm informed that "this type of operation exercised by Pure Leisure gives them a kickback from the insurance company who may not be aware of what's taking place prior to their involvement". According to my Oxford dictionary, a kickback is described as a "payment for collaboration – especially for illicit profit".

3. REPAIRS AND RENEWALS

During our first winter on the park we suffered two burst pipes in the water system, due to a sudden unexpected heavy frost. In respect of the repair work I received an invoice, enclosed herein, from Pure Leisure Number 21 for an exact amount totalling £89.00 which comprises their "product description – repair to burst pipes", i.e. "unit price £75.7447, net amount £75.74, V.A.T. amount £13.26" all adding up to a nice round figure.

A6 Yealand Redmayne
Nr. Carnforth
Lancs
LA5 9RN

Telephone   01524 781918
Fax   01524 782243
VAT Number 514 3195 67

pure leisure
GROUP

Mr & Mrs S Cooper

Invoice   21
Date   31/07/2006
Account No. FCOO255

Quantity	Product Description	Unit Price	Net Amount	VAT Amount
1.00	Repair to Burst Pipes	75.7447	75.74	13.26

PLEASE SEND PAYMENTS TO:-

Pure Leisure
Fellend Caravan Park
Slackhead Road
Hale
Milnthorpe
LA7 7BS

Net Amount	75.74
VAT Amount	13.26
Carriage	0.00
Invoice Total	89.00

Still wearing my rose-tinted glasses (for the last time) I settled the account without quibble. We were away from the caravan at the time the work was carried out, which was in 2006.

Some time later, I was chatting to the Park's handyman and mentioned if he'd had any difficulty in accessing the pipes in question. He informed me that he found the two bursts without any bother and he'd completed the task within twenty minutes – "A doddle".

Not too long ago the topic of conversation turned to this area of Pure Leisure's activities when a chum of mine, still residing on the park and whom we still meet up with on a regular basis, told me of an incident regarding an electrical problem in his caravan which had now been, in a fashion, resolved.

My friend is a retired electrician, having run his own firm in Lancashire for many years. The reason he approached Pure Leisure to rectify the problem was the fact that he did not possess the correct modern adjusting tool to carry out the "five minute job" - and that was the time it actually took.

He duly received an invoice in excess of ninety pounds. Prior to payment, he informed Pure Leisure, he would need a detailed break-down i.e. labour, parts etc. Several requests proved fruitless.

In an attempt to activate a positive response from Pure Leisure he deliberately did not pay his site fee deposit when it became due. As expected they came onto him up in arms asking why, after an unblemished payment record over seven years on the park. So he re-iterated his requests for a breakdown etc. and was advised by the Director of Communications, no less, a Mr. Green that the company could not furnish him with a breakdown as after six months they did not keep records.

Whilst he then paid the site fee deposit he's never heard another thing regarding the unpaid account. Why didn't I take my friend's stance? In time, as you will see however, I did just that – and with what repercussions.

4. A DISGUISED THREAT?

The common focal point for residents collecting their mail at Fell End was obviously at the reception desk. The service in this respect became intolerable after a certain lady, whom I will name as 'Miss E.' was transferred to Pure Leisure's Head Office. Upon her return however matters reverted back to the level we were used to. I remember in particular asking her to look at the postal system which had become a 'free for all', by which I mean the mail was received and just tossed willy-nilly onto the counter for all to pick and see. This created a potentially uncomfortable situation regarding security. Miss E. immediately put into operation a simple but effective system to everyone's relief and satisfaction.

I've mentioned the foregoing to assure the reader at the outset of this story of my respect and admiration for Miss E., particularly in view of what was to take place some time later, a respect which I have for her to this day.

One day and out of the blue I espied Miss E. lingering outside our caravan. She willingly accepted my offer of a cup of tea and duly stayed for well over an hour, during which time she revealed matters concerning the owner of Fell End Park which left me utterly flabbergasted.

Immediately after Miss E. left I scribbled down the nitty-gritty details of her revelations, which are as follows:

1pm to 2pm approx.
Monday 4.1.10

Conversation between Miss E., Margaret and I resulting in following comments to Margaret and me from Miss E., regarding John Morphet, the owner of Fell End.

"John Morphet's wife and child threatened with kidnap note left at their house. £25,000 demanded which had to be left in the garage. This he paid. He has contacts and blackmailers later suffered broken knee-caps". Miss E. further stated that: "he always paid off any person who threatened to reveal his unlawful actions. A very dangerous man – be very sure of your case against him before continuing."

I still, to this day, cannot really bring myself to believe a word of Miss E's disclosures. I promised myself however that in writing this book there had to be no holding back, "warts and all" as they say.

Initially I thought how big-hearted and indeed brave Miss E. was being, in disclosing these explosive allegations, then I slowly began to have my doubts. How did she know of my ongoing battle with Pure Leisure regarding the electricity overcharging, and why should she be so concerned as to my well-being over this matter which did not affect her one iota?

Her visit of the fourth of January 2010 was just over three weeks after my letter of ultimatum to Pure Leisure regarding the electricity fraud (which included two weeks of the festive season), wherein I stated my intentions of seeking legal advice.

Despite these factors of doubt I have come to the conclusion that Miss E. was acting under orders designed to frighten me off. Her visit, I now believed, was actually a veiled threat.

I understand that some time later Miss E. was dismissed from her employ. She has since refused to answer or return my telephone calls to her home and appears to ignore my wife in the streets of Kendal. Again, I believe her actions are due to 'extended orders'.

Like many, many others who have come into contact with Fell End Caravan Park, this nice lady's life, I suspect, has been changed: and not for the good.

5. NAÏVETY? + ENVY? = EGG ON FACE?

I'm confident one will understand why I began to take a deeper interest than most in certain matters concerning Fell End Caravan Park. On one occasion, my interest reached as far as a local newspaper's readers' correspondence columns. This instance concerned a letter from the Fell End Park's owner, the subject of which related to the Skelwith Fold Caravan Park which was situated in the Lake District, a few miles from Ambleside – dare I say it? – "the jewel in the crown'. This letter, in the 15th October 2009 edition of the paper, concerned a diatribical message to Mr Henry Wild, the owner of Skelwith Fold.

Suffice to say letters of reaction to the newspaper from both the public and two highly respectable local park owners, Chris Barron and Matt Brindle of Bigland Hall Caravan Park, and Henry Wild himself completely flattened Fell End Park's onslaught. These replies were not answered. There *was* no answer, but an apology perhaps? No.

However, you may have already gathered I am about to add my two pennyworth. It being not as much in defence of Henry Wild but in support of the truth against deliberate misleading statements, some of which were to me, a disguised attempt to promote business interests including those of Fell End Park.

Coinciding at the time of the aforementioned, work was taking place at Fell End in destroying a Woodland children's park and play area, it eventually being replaced with what I can only describe as wooden boxes. They are known as Pods.

They do not possess any facilities whatsoever apart from an electric heater affixed to one of the walls. They are rented out on a nightly basis, the charge being £25.00 per night, and cater for up to four people. To any observer they are utterly basic units, to me, creating a health and safety risk, and in no way, in Fell End

Owner's words: "address the quality and diversity of existing homes" which he wishes (in his letter to Henry Wild) to promote in respect of all homes.

The initial batch of these pods were put up without local authority planning consent. The park manager at the time, Eric, reported this state of affairs to South Lakeland District Council and then resigned. I found him a fair and genuine person and he said this was the final straw at the end of a catalogue of unsavoury incidents he'd experienced – ones which he could no longer stomach.

My Oxford English Dictionary describes a pod as "a compartment suspended under an aircraft for equipment etc."

Regarding Mr. Morphet's criticism of the colour white shown in the newspaper's picture of one sole caravan at Skelwith Fold i.e. "One would have thought that, at the very least, units should be furnished in environmentally sensitive green rather than the shiny white of the example in the background of your photograph of Skelwith Park" I would comment as follows:

The caravan pictured is in fact cream in colour with a matt finish. In any case, what is wrong with shiny? On the 15th October 2009 after a careful walk around Fell End Park I telephoned Henry Wild and informed him there were 34 non-green units in residence. I couldn't help but admire his gracious reaction which, I suppose, is becoming of the chairman of the British Holiday and Home Parks Association responsible to almost 3,000 park businesses – a real, true chairman.

6. FELL END'S RULES AND REGULATIONS

You will observe my solicitors later saying "a team of coach and horses could be driven through these rules and regulations". However being a layman in respect of matters relating to law I humbly put forward a few of my personal observations regarding the above.

Rule 13 states: "The Park is licenced as a holiday park and not a residential park. No holiday home shall be occupied as a person's sole or main place of residence".

A good number of holiday homes were (and still are to my knowledge) occupied as the sole/main place of residence. I had direct knowledge of this during my six years on the park – my home was one of them. I came across more than a dozen instances which contradicted the ruling. Furthermore, the Park's management was fully aware of this taking place. Indeed it appeared to me that the Park encouraged contravention of this ruling by way of the following:

Rule 13.2 states: "The Park should not be your mailing address and should not be used for the delivery of post".

In contradiction of this they had a postal system at reception set up purposely for the delivery of mail. Indeed, residents enjoyed having their own mailing slot. This facility was obviously appreciated by us 'full-timers' and the Park knew it.

On the other hand, utterly contradictory and puzzling as it may appear a neighbour of mine on the park, in complaining bitterly about a particular matter, was threatened with removal when it was pointed out to him that he was using his caravan as his sole/main residence. I believe an ulterior motive was the reason for their threat. It must be borne in mind my neighbour had been in occupancy for over ten years. His caravan was like new and he probably had the most desirable plot on the park. You will quickly see through their motive upon reading through chapters thirteen and fifteen in this book – "The Sales and Buy-backs".

Rule 1.5 states: "The Park cannot be used as a base from which to travel to and from work on a regular basis". Prior to my retirement and for almost a year I ignored this ruling. The park management, as with other residents doing likewise, 'looked the other way'.

Rule 3.2 states: "Pitch fees are reviewed on an annual basis. Pure Leisure will endeavour to give you three months' notice in writing of any increase in pitch fees". During my stay on the Park pitch fees increased every year. There was never any notice or explanation. Furthermore this situation was evident with all residents.

Rule 3.4 states: "Local authority rates and service charges are included with the pitch fees". Each and every year I was invoiced with:
1. "Site fees for season" and
2. "Rates for season".

No breakdown as to how the rates were calculated was ever included e.g. I was charged rates for the season from the 1st March 2011 to the 15th January 2012 the sum of £225.00. The park was charged, as a matter of interest, the sum of £51,960 payable in 2011/12 in respect of non-domestic rates by the South Lakeland District Council – but more of this later! I am led to believe that in 2014 the Government made law that these rates now attracted V.A.T. at 20% which was shown on the residents' invoice without any forewarning or explanation.

I often asked myself why the Park did not adhere to, but indeed aided and abetted in contravening their very own rules and regulations. Eventually I came to the conclusion that strict enforcement would cramp their potential for maximum income.

Later in the book, under the chapter "Sales and Buy Backs" I refer to rule 4 which comes under the Park's heading "Holiday Home Sales". This is where the 'real serious business' in the book commences.

Enclosed herein you will find the Fell End Park's actual current rules and regulations. I feel these are worthy of your (may I suggest) critical gaze. Apart from several rulings I have highlighted previously, Rule 19.5 you may find of interest or indeed puzzling. Surely any leisure park worth its salt and by the very nature of its business would expect only messages of praise? Could the Park be existing in a state of apprehension of what might be (or has already been) revealed? I am, of course, referring to any actions taken by the park of a nature detrimental to its residents. Whilst I have mentioned various rulings previously, they being relevant to the book's progress, I find ruling 19.5 odd in so much as the inclusion of the word "tradesmen". Why not therefore include say, clerks, taxi drivers, musicians and so on?

FELL END CARAVAN PARK – Slackhead Road – Milnthorpe Cumbria – LA7 7BP – Tel 015395 62122

ANNUAL SITE LICENCE CONDITIONS and GENERAL SITE RULES

Introduction and Summary

This agreement permits you to station a holiday home on a park and to occupy it for holiday and recreational purposes. This permission is personal to you and may not be assigned or transferred to another person. The permission comes to an end when you sell the holiday home to a third party (including family members). Please note that this is a legally binding agreement.

All persons using the park must comply with the following rules, which are necessary in order to maintain standards and conditions and to ensure that all occupiers enjoy the benefits of the park. Payment in full or in part and/or entry onto the park shall be deemed to be acceptance of these conditions/rules and as such, form part of the agreement for the occupancy of a pitch on the park.

The expression "you" refers to the Holiday Home owner/occupier and "Pure Leisure" refers to the sole trader business of Mr J C Morphet, the owner of the park. The Pure Leisure office is at South Lakeland House, A6, Yealand Redmayne, Carnforth, Lancs LA5 9RN. You are reminded that breach of these rules is a breach of your Licence Agreement and may result in termination of the Licence Agreement. The offer of an Annual Site Licence is granted subject to the holiday home being maintained in good condition, compliance with the terms and conditions of the licence as outlined below, general site rules being observed and the reasonable behaviour of the holiday home owner and all other users of the holiday home.

1. Site Licence and Park

1.1 All occupiers at the Park must comply with the conditions attached to the Site Licence issued by South Lakeland District Council, which are on display in Reception
1.2 The park comprises of Fell End Caravan Park, Slackhead Road, Milnthorpe and includes all facilities now or presently on site and maintained by Pure Leisure
1.3 The park is licenced as a holiday park and not a residential park. No holiday home shall be occupied as a person's sole or main place of residence.
1.4 As a condition for the site licence from time to time you may be asked to provide Pure Leisure with evidence of your permanent home. Failure to provide such evidence may result in you being asked to vacate your holiday home.
1.5 Pitch numbers must remain visible
1.6 Leisure Passes will be issued for up to four people in a two bedroom holiday home and up to six people in a three bedroom holiday home.

2. The Season

2.1 The park is open for occupation between 9am on the 6th February and 5pm on the 15th January each year.

3. Payments

3.1 Site fees are payable in two instalments, £800 deposit on the 31st October and the balance by 1st March for the forthcoming season and are non-transferable.
No holiday home may be occupied after 1st March unless the site fees are paid in full.
3.2 Pitch fees are reviewed on an annual basis. Pure Leisure will endeavour to give you three months notice in writing of any increase to pitch fees, having regard to any changes in the cost of living, sums spent by Pure Leisure on the park and or its facilities, changes in the costs of salaries/wages paid to our staff, changes in the length of the Season or any other relevant factor.
3.3 No holiday home may be occupied unless the site fee is paid in full.
3.4 Local Authority Rates and service charges are invoiced with the pitch fees.
3.5 Interest will be charged from the due date on all overdue accounts at the rate of 3% above the Bank Base Rate.
3.6 Electricity charges will be payable within 14 days of demand. Charges will be based on the guidelines issued by OFGEM
3.7 Failure to settle an overdue account will result in disconnection of supplies and a charge will be made for reconnection.

4. Holiday Home Sales

4.1 The sale of all new holiday homes onto the park will be conducted solely by Pure Leisure.
4.2 Re-sale of holiday homes – the holiday homeowner must first offer the holiday home to Pure Leisure at a fair market price. Pure Leisure will have 7 days to accept your offer of sale. Should the price of the holiday home decrease, it must again be offered to Pure Leisure on the same terms.
4.3 Static caravans are sold with the licence period of up to 15 years from the date of purchase when new. Any variation to this rule will only be valid if received in writing from Pure Leisure.
4.4 All holiday homes will be subject to an annual review as to fitness to remain on the park. If the holiday home is found, in the judgement of Pure Leisure, to be unsightly, in a poor state of repair or unsafe then Pure Leisure reserve the right to ask the owner to make good the defect or at its sole discretion ask the owner to remove it from park
4.5 Holiday homes purchased as private sales may not be re-offered as a private sale without express permission of Pure Leisure
4.6 In the event of Pure Leisure not wishing to purchase the holiday home, permission to sell must be obtained in writing from Pure Leisure. Permission to sell on the park will normally be granted to the holiday homeowner upon completion with Pure Leisure of a Private Sale Agreement.
4.7 You agree to conduct the private sales transaction through our office and appoint us as your agent for that purpose.
4.8 Any holiday homeowner may not introduce as a prospective purchaser any persons who have previously approached Pure Leisure directly with a view to purchasing a holiday home from Pure Leisure, nor may the seller sell to any existing Pure Leisure customer. You agree to allow us to approve your prospective buyer by seeking suitable references and carrying out the enquiries we consider appropriate. If we wish to, we may require a meeting with your buyer in person. Such approval will not be unreasonably withheld.
4.9 Full details, both as to the identity of the proposed new owner and as to the conditions of the sale must be fully disclosed to Pure Leisure prior to the completion of any sale. The full gross proceeds of the sale must be transacted through the Park Office

4.10 No holiday home may be marketed unless all outstanding account balances are zero.
4.11 Pure Leisure will finalise the financial arrangements and pay to the seller of the holiday home the balance due, after deducting 15% commission plus VAT, based on the fair market value together with any outstanding ledger balance which may be due to Pure Leisure
4.12 Pure Leisure reserves the right to relocate any holiday home to an alternative pitch upon any sale or transfer of ownership.
4.13 Any owner who wishes to remove a holiday home from the park must give Pure Leisure 14 days notice of removal. Pure Leisure must carry out disconnection of the services and make ready to remove. A reasonable charge will be made for this service. All monies due to Pure Leisure must be paid before the holiday home is removed from the park.

5. Occupancy

5.1 No holiday home may be sublet on the park.
5.2 When a holiday home is to be occupied overnight by persons other than the owner they must report to the park office and sign in on arrival (or as soon as possible if arriving outside park office hours).
5.3 The park management, at their discretion, may refuse admission to persons with good reason.
5.4 No holiday home shall be used for sleeping a number of persons greater than the number for which it was designed
5.5 It is your responsibility to ensure that your visitors and occupiers of your holiday home adhere to the park rules.
5.6 Please respect the privacy of other holiday homeowners and keep noise to a minimum with absolute quiet between 12 midnight and 0800 hours.
5.7 During the closed season from the 16th January to the 28th February, no overnight occupation of the holiday home is allowed. If visiting the holiday home during this period, for security reasons, please report to the Park Office on arrival & departure. Visits are restricted to daylight hours between 10.00am & 4.00pm.
5.8 Occupiers are advised to remove all valuables from the holiday home during the closed period & to place movable items. e.g. outdoor furniture, steps, cylinders etc. inside the holiday home.
5.9 Pure Leisure reserves the right to terminate all services to the holiday home in the closed season – i.e. electricity & water - and may do so without prior notice. Pure Leisure is unable to guarantee continuous provision of water/electric supply to holiday homes and you are advised to take precautions with electrical dependant equipment. (i.e. not leave freezers etc... overstocked in case of power interruption) Guidance for the water supply is outlined in point 8.1.

6. Motor Vehicles

6.1 Only one vehicle may be parked at the holiday home unless provided with hard standing for two vehicles.
6.2 Only private vehicles may be brought onto or parked on the park. No commercial vehicles, vans, wagons, boats, trailers or motor homes are to be brought onto or parked on the park without the prior permission of the park office. This permission should not unreasonably be withheld.
6.3 Drivers are requested to observe a 5mph speed limit at all times and observe all road signs and the traffic management system in force. The same requirements as on the Public Highways apply on the park e.g. vehicle fitness for purpose and safety, qualified drivers only, no drink driving, wearing of crash helmets etc.
6.4 Vehicles must be kept to authorised parking spaces and to the roads, which must not be obstructed.
6.5 Driving or parking on the grass is not permitted.
6.6 We permit cars onto the park for the purposes of access to the holiday home only and they are not to be used to drive around the park
6.7 Pedestrians must be given priority
6.8 In the interests of safety and to comply with the Road Traffic Act 1988 the use of Mini Motos, Quad Bikes, Trial Bikes, Electric Powered or Petrol Driven Scooters are not permitted within the boundaries of the park. Skateboards, Roller Blades and Roller Skates are also prohibited from use on the park. Cycles may be used with care and must only be used during daylight hours.
6.9 Only vehicles taxed and insured for use on a public road may be kept at the park and we will remove any disused or broken down vehicles for which you will be charged.
6.10 You are not permitted to give anyone else driving lessons at the park and we do not permit learner drivers to drive on the park
6.11 Washing of vehicles on park is not permitted

7. Building and ground works

7.1 Each holiday home is restricted to one storage box of a type and size, which we approve in writing. Such approval will not be unreasonably withheld.
7.2 External structures may be added to the holiday home e.g. a veranda or balcony only with the written approval of the park. Porches, walkways and carports are not permitted.
7.3 You must not install slabs or paving without first obtaining written permission from Pure Leisure.
7.4 Pitches must be kept clean, tidy and free from litter at all times.
7.5 Fences are NOT permitted around pitches.
7.6 The park will be responsible for general grass cutting but individual pitch occupiers will be responsible for ensuring that lawns are kept cut and flowerbeds and pathways on the pitch are kept in proper repair, neat and tidy at all times, including the removal of weeds and rubbish from beneath the holiday home. If Pure Leisure is impeded from carrying out normal site maintenance or the holiday homeowner fails to maintain their pitch to a satisfactory standard Pure Leisure shall be entitled to recover the cost of remedial work. Pure Leisure reserves the right to trim or remove plant material. Plants, bushes or trees that are the property of Pure Leisure may NOT be removed by the holiday homeowner. No pruning of trees may be carried out except with the prior permission of Pure Leisure.
7.7 Garden furniture must be placed on the pitch so as to not impede grass cutting undertaken by Pure Leisure personnel.
7.8 Any homeowners wishing to erect a small plan garden or patio must first make an individual application to Pure Leisure. Permission will not be unreasonably withheld.

8. Winter Water Drainage, Annual Gas Safety Test and Periodic Electrical Installation Test

8.1 In order to safeguard against frost damage we recommend that the water system of every vacant holiday home be drained. A charge of £150 will be made for costly water consumption due to frost damage. The park office can arrange this service and will be pleased to provide further details including charges upon request.
8.2 Homeowners are reminded of the advisability of holding a current annual Gas Safety Test Certificate. The park office can arrange this service and will be pleased to provide further details including charges upon request. From time to time you may be asked to provide evidence of certification.

8.3 Pure Leisure is responsible for the periodic testing of the electrical installation of the park up to the consumer unit only. Homeowners are advised to have the electrical installation of the holiday home checked by a NICEIC registered electrician every three years for holiday homes less than 10 years old, or annually for holiday homes more than 10 years old. The park office can arrange for this and will be pleased to provide further details including charges upon request. Any additional electrical work carried out in and about the holiday home must have a certificate by a registered NICEIC/NAPIT/ECA electrician, which should be made available to the park office on request.

9. Holiday Home Rules

9.1 It is the owners responsibility to keep the holiday home in a good state of repair and condition both visually and structurally and so as to retain its mobility and in a safe, habitable state including the repair and maintenance of all installations and appliances and undertaking and /or commissioning of all relevant periodic safety checks.
9.2 All loose materials and equipment must be secured to prevent damage in harsh weather conditions. Toys, barbeques etc must be stored out of sight when the holiday home is not occupied.
9.3 Walls, fences and any obstruction to the access of the base are NOT permitted though skirts provided by Pure Leisure or those approved by Pure Leisure in writing are permitted.
9.4 The exterior colour of the holiday home may not be changed.
9.5 Any alterations to the inside of any holiday home will affect its resale value and could render it void for sale on the park.
9.6 All domestic refuse must be placed in appropriate bins located around the park.
9.7 Washing lines or rotary dryers are not permitted and must not be erected on pitches. A laundrette is available on park for your use.
9.8 Children under 14 years old must be left unattended in your holiday home at any time.
9.9 Children must not be allowed to make a nuisance of themselves on other people's pitches. Children must play on their own pitch or any dedicated children's play area. The playing of football and other hard ball sports like cricket or golf is prohibited.
9.10 The conduct of children is deemed to be the responsibility of parents/guardians at all times.
9.11 No nappies, tea bags or other deleterious matter must be put down the toilet or drains. Any blockage to the drainage system caused by a homeowner may be charged at the cost of making good. Bleach or other harmful chemicals must not be used in the toilets or drainage system. Such use may cause serious damage to the private sewerage treatment plant. The use of deleterious chemicals is traceable and accordingly Pure Leisure gives notice of its intention to recover costs.
9.12 Bird feeders are restricted to 1 small feeder per pitch at the discretion of the park manager as they can attract rodents.
9.13 Hosepipes are not permitted on park.

10. Insurance

10.1 Homeowners are required to insure the holiday home against all usual risks including fire, storm damage, property owner's liability, public liability, employee's liability and against third party liability. This can be arranged with the park office or with a regulated insurer. Proof that insurance is in force must be produced to Pure Leisure annually on inception or renewal of policy.

11. Fire Safety

11.1 All homeowners need to be aware of the procedure for dealing with fire and other emergencies on the park. The greatest care must be taken to prevent outbreaks of fire. Fire fighting equipment is provided at strategic locations around the park.
11.2 Every holiday home must be equipped with adequate fire fighting equipment including as a minimum, a 1kg fire extinguisher, fire blanket and smoke alarm. All equipment must be maintained in good condition and in full working order.
11.3 Fire extinguishers must not be used for any improper purpose.
11.4 It is the owner's responsibility to ensure that all occupiers of the holiday home are familiar with the location of the Fire Points and the contents of the Fire Notices at each point.
11.5 No multi fuel or wood burning stoves are permitted within the holiday homes.
11.6 No fuels or combustible materials other than LPG containers may be stored on the park.
11.7 The use of portable paraffin heaters and open fires is prohibited. Barbeques may be used but not within the holiday home or on or within close proximity of the decking. Further, disposable barbeques may not be used directly on grassed areas.

12. Pets

12.1 Pets are permitted on the park but must be kept under strict control at all times. Dogs must be kept on a lead at all times. Dog owners not exercising proper control will be asked to remove their dogs from the park. Dogs banned under the Dangerous Dogs Act 1991 are not permitted on park. Pet owners are required to clean up after their pets.
12.2 Pets must not be left unattended inside holiday homes.

13. Office Hours/Mail

13.1 The park office will be open at all times displayed at the entrance. Members of staff are available at the times stated. Only in emergencies can the park managers be contacted outside these hours. Please respect the privacy of the park managers.
13.2 The park address should not be your main mailing address and should not be used for the delivery of post.
13.3 Telephone messages will not be taken by the park office except in an emergency.

14. Other Matters

14.1 No firearms, explosives, offensive weapons or other items likely to give offence may be carried, kept or used on the park.
14.2 No drugs or other substances harmful to health or social well-being may be brought onto or used on the park.
14.3 Pure Leisure reserves the right to refuse admission to the park or to any facilities of the park. Permission is not to be unreasonably withheld.
14.4 Pure Leisure shall use reasonable endeavours to ensure the availability of all amenities advertised in its brochure or otherwise but shall not be liable in respect of non-availability.
14.5 No commercial enterprise or business activity may take place on the park without the express written permission of Pure Leisure.
14.6 No holiday home may bear any advertising matter other than the manufacturers name and no notices may be displayed on the park without the prior permission of the park managers.
14.7 Any major works/repairs must have the prior authorisation of Pure Leisure. Permission for such works will not be unreasonably withheld.
14.8 All holiday homes must have a spare/reserve gas cylinder at all times. The park office will advise of the arrangements for replenishing supplies of bottled gas.

14.9 Keys – please ensure that a spare set of keys for your holiday home are lodged with the park office for use in emergencies. Details re security devices and routines for isolation should also be provided.

14.10 Requests for chargeable services such as repairs and gas supplies must be made to the park office and NOT to individual employees. Please note that only emergencies will be dealt with outside of normal working hours.

15. Moving the Holiday Home

15.1 Pure Leisure is allowed to move the holiday home for the purposes of redevelopment and/or maintenance of the park. In such instances Pure Leisure will give the Owner three months notice in writing. If the holiday home is to be moved because of an emergency or because of works to be carried out over which Pure Leisure has no control we will give you as much notice as we can. Pure Leisure will be responsible for all reasonable costs incurred in moving the holiday home.

15.2 Following redevelopment Pure Leisure is entitled to return the holiday home to its original pitch or to site it permanently on another pitch. If, as a consequence of redevelopment, the original pitch is less pleasant or if the move is permanent Pure Leisure will offer an alternative satisfactory pitch. In determining the pleasantness of the original pitch as a result of redevelopment, loss of view and proximity of vehicular traffic will be considered.

16. Visitors and Tradesmen

16.1 If you have arranged for visitors or tradesmen to enter the park, you must inform the park office the day before the visit with:
  a) The name of the visitor/tradesperson or delivery
  b) The name of the person they are visiting and the pitch number

In the interests of security, failure to provide this information, in advance, will result in entry being refused. Unless pre-arranged, visitors should park in the main car park and walk to the holiday home.

17. Loss or Damage

17.1 Unless negligent or in breach of duty caused by Pure Leisure, its employees or agents, Pure Leisure will not be held liable for any loss or damage to any person, holiday home, motor vehicle, equipment or other property except for an act of deliberate or wilful damage.

18. Termination of the Agreement

18.1 The Licence may come to an end in any of the following ways;
  18.1.1 By you giving Pure Leisure two months notice in writing of your wish to end it
  18.1.2 Because the Licence Period has passed
  18.1.3 By the sale of the holiday home or you losing title to it
  18.1.4 By Pure Leisure taking steps to terminate because you have broken your obligations under this Agreement.

18.2 Pure Leisure reserves the right to terminate the licence to occupy a pitch as a consequence of a serious breach of agreement that is not capable of remedy by the holiday homeowner, upon serving reasonable written notice at the last known address of the occupier to that effect specifying the breach and the occupier's rights in relation thereto. If you are in breach of your obligations under this agreement, which are capable of being remedied, we may write giving you notice specifying the breach and giving you the opportunity to remedy it within a reasonable time. If you do not comply with that notice Pure Leisure is entitled to write to you to end the Licence Agreement and require you to remove the holiday home from the park within one month.

18.3 If the Licence Agreement comes to an end you must remove the holiday home and all other property of yours from the Park within one month of the termination of this Agreement, however it comes about.

18.4 Pure Leisure is entitled to make a reasonable charge for disconnecting the holiday home from services and preparing it for transport away from the Park.

18.5 If following termination of the Licence Agreement you fail to arrange the removal of the holiday home, Pure Leisure is entitled to do so and recover the cost of removal from the disposal of the holiday home as it sees fit.

18.6 On termination of this agreement or leaving the park, whichever is the later, an owner is entitled to a refund of site fees on the following terms.

If before the end of March	70%
If before the end of July	40%
If after the end of July	Zero

19. General

19.1 Use of the park and its facilities is conditional upon these rules being strictly adhered to and all persons conducting themselves with due regard for Pure Leisure, its employees and the well-being and comfort of others.

19.2 All persons, including holiday homeowners, their guests and tradesmen must act in a courteous and considerate manner towards our staff and contractors. Rudeness, verbal abuse or insults will be considered a serious breach of these rules and is unacceptable.

19.3 All persons, including holiday homeowners, their guests and tradesmen must not act in any way, which interferes with or causes prejudice to Pure Leisure business.

19.4 All persons, including holiday homeowners, their guests and tradesmen must not make misleading statements or take other action, which may lead others to consider that they are dealing with a representative of Pure Leisure or are authorised on Pure Leisure's behalf.

19.5 All persons, including holiday homeowners, their guests and tradesmen will not use social media of any kind, in a way that is harmful or prejudicial to Pure Leisure, its business or employees.

7. HEALTH AND SAFETY

During my two year search for a park suitable for our requirements it became obvious that any park of note would possess an automated barrier at its entrance. Without one all and sundry could come and go at will. At Fell End they did particularly, as its entrance was adjacent to a public thoroughfare which exacerbated this worrying state of affairs.

At the beginning of the drive which led to the majority of the static caravans there was a stretch where it had collapsed. However whether car, caravan or pedestrian it could be negotiated with care. It remained in that state for at least two years.

Underground cabling took place twice in as many years – one of these instances involved electricity. The cable was laid about nine inches below the surface. I ruefully took stock of a separate electric cable line, half of which protruded as it crossed part of my garden. I had to be extremely careful when planting, weeding, etc.. However after a while I became used to this grey, plastic snake-like cable, humped in places, crossing the land, its destination unknown, I thought, to anybody. My neighbours however, were greatly concerned that none of the park staff involved possessed any electrical qualifications whatsoever. After digging a shallow trench to cater for a T.V. line it meant having to cross the gravelled area separating my caravan from two other homes with care. As with many other of their 'digs' on the park, what they had excavated was just tossed back on, resulting in a ten yard long, one foot wide, rubbled mound. No heavy roller, tarmacadam etc.. That was it. Job Done.

Litter bins. You've guessed it, invariably overflowing particularly after weekends, bank holidays etc. there was no immediate on-site attention. They could be left for days until the official disposal unit arrived. Several bins were virtually at the site entrance – first impressions do not always count, do they?

A site resident, although wishing to remain anonymous, provided me with the following factual happenings. One winter's day the park had run out of gas bottles, resulting of course in no heating supply. The park manager proudly came up with his solution: "leave your (electric) cooker on".

He was present when Matt Morphet (responsible for the smooth running of the commercial workings on the park, e.g. electrics, water, sewage) who, upon being shown the park's diagrams, plans and maps etc. detailing the path of every pipe and cable, he nonchalantly tossed them aside. A night/day record book received similar treatment.

Due to ignorance of how to work a valve controlled water system, it was switched off at times to alleviate the build-up of pressure. I was lead to understand this created a big health risk. He was once advised by the park manager at the time a caravan caught fire that in a case of this nature water must *not* be used, only foam from an extinguisher. Surprisingly enough this manager enjoyed many years of employment without any guidance or supervision. This information was divulged to me in strict confidence by an ex-employee of the company

The park's written site ruling number 11.4 states:

"It is the owner's (Fell End's) responsibility to ensure that all occupiers of the holiday homes are familiar with the location of the fire points, and the contents of the fire notices at each point".

As with myself, I never came across any resident who had been furnished with this information. A current resident, upon my request in May 2014, confirmed there were approximately thirty fire points on the park. Each one contained a fire extinguisher and fire blanket. It always amazed me that there wasn't a hose and reel anywhere to be found, nor any water availability directions.

The final part of our route home, which was in excess of one hundred yards, did not possess any lighting. In the dark, if a certain park employee had driven by a tricky situation could have developed. You see for many years in the course of his duties he drove a motorised vehicle around the park without even possessing a provisional (L) driving license.

For the past three to four years the site manager has lived four miles from the park. This left a void in respect of night security.

For a period of time a site resident was co-opted in to answer any outside telephone calls, the park's line being put through to his caravan. He was paid a meagre sum, a pittance in effect. Despite this state of affairs he was eventually relieved of his duties, only finding out when discovering his monthly payment did not appear on his bank statement.

Referring back to my earlier observations regarding waste disposal bins, the following has now been brought to my attention by way of the park's current (2014/2015) rules and regulations. They state:

Clause 9.12 states - "Bird feeders are now restricted to one small feeder per pitch at the discretion of the park manager as they can attract rodents" (This description would include the lovely rare red squirrels by the way). The ruling comes after over twenty years of their knowledge on the park. I suggest overflowing waste bins – not bird feeders – are the main cause of creating a health hazard, i.e. encouraging the presence of vermin, namely rats. I do not see them anyway having much chance in competing with birds in getting to any spillage in time for these tiny seeds. What, therefore, is the real reason for this ruling? Should a plague of rats surface can this now be blamed on the park holiday home residents instead of the overflowing waste bins and/or possibly the park's sewerage systems if on occasions they can't cope?

Nevertheless, in this instance it is reassuring and gratifying to know some concern is felt for the Park's human residents by the management. Credit when it's due I say.

INTERLUDE (PAUSE FOR THOUGHT)

Once again, Christmas is approaching. In the compilation of this book I cease writing during the festive season to give as much time and love as possible to my family, friends and indeed whoever I meet. Just being normal I suppose. However, this brought myself to thinking; how can people in this World, who perpetuate ongoing actions of deceit throughout their yearly working life, and in doing so hurting their fellow mankind, come or be able to genuinely bestow this Christian spirit on those around them?

8. THE "SUPPLY" OF WATER AND ELECTRICITY

Pure Leisure's ruling number 5.9 states:

"Pure Leisure is unable to guarantee continuous provision of water/electric supply to holiday homes and you are advised to take precautions with electrical dependent equipment (i.e. not leave freezers etc. overstocked in case of power interruption)"

Evidently this new ruling (2014/2015 season) has been implemented to insure Pure Leisure against any claims. It leads me to believe they will not invest in systems which prevent the regular 'on-off' water and electric scenario, which was happening from eight years ago at least two to three times a week on average at my holiday home – holiday home?

The Park's 2014/2015 annual site licence conditions and regulations now also state the following:

Rule 8.1 – "In order to safeguard against frost damage, we recommend that the water system of every vacant holiday home be drained, a charge of £150 will be made for costly water consumption due to frost damage. The Park Office can arrange this service and will be pleased to provide further details including charges upon request." Each time frost damage took place surely you would not be charged £150.00?

A resident has informed me the current 2015 drain-down charge is £60.00 plus V.A.T.. I am not a practically-minded person by any means, particularly 'round the house'. More of a Frank Spencer, (Some Mothers Do Have 'Em). Nevertheless, after tuition which followed my first frost damage repair costs, I could manage this draining task each year, just prior to the six weeks 'off park' regulation, in about half an hour, when nobody was looking.

In contrast to the aforementioned charge of £150 by the Fell End Park my current annual bill, shown herein by United Utilities in respect of *total* waste water usage, equates to 57p per day, or £206.94 per annum.

The Park's obvious reluctance to invest has therefore created a sub-standard electrical system not fit for purpose. This provides knock-on detrimental effects as follows:
1. Units could be degraded to the class of "un-merchantable quality" therefore possibly unfit for sale. Is this the law?
2. When purchasing your caravan, be it new or used, you are in effect being indirectly "short-changed". Does the contravention of the trades description act apply here?
3. The manufacturer's concerns particularly in respect of new units must be ones of unease (that is, if they knew).
4. The caravan purchaser (resident) has paid anything up to £60,000 for something possessing a potential and fundamental fault. One which could greatly affect the main reason to purchase – a care-free, relaxed, comfortable, holiday life-style.

Should you have cared to reflect on my writings so far I'm sure you may be coming to the conclusion that whatever, wherever and whenever a holiday home owner requires a service, either because of necessity or otherwise, there is no 'hiding place' from the Park's determination to exercise and implement financial penalties of an excessive and greed-filled nature. If you haven't, I can guarantee it *will* become a forgone conclusion, well before the end of the book.

Information

2014 Special Discount
You will see a credit on this bill entitled '2014 Special Discount'. This is a one-off discount of £5.00 which is helping to reduce the amount you need to pay towards your bill this year. This is our way of helping customers at a time when household budgets are stretched.

For further details visit
unitedutilities.com/goodnews

How am I billed?
Your bills are based on the Rateable Value (RV) of your home. We times the unit cost by each £1 of the property's rateable value.

Water standing charge
This fixed charge makes sure costs for delivering water, sending bills and dealing with enquiries, are shared fairly between customers.

Water RV charge
This charge is for the cost to supply clean water to your home.

Wastewater RV charge
This charge is for collecting your used water before cleaning it and returning it safely to the environment. It also covers the cost of taking away rainwater that drains from your property (surface water) and the public highway.

You may be entitled to a reduction in your charges if the surface water does not drain into the sewer system.

For more information visit
unitedutilities.com/surface-water-drainage

Can I change my Rateable Value (RV)?
The RV for your property cannot be changed. It was set by the Valuation Office up to 1990 based on the size, type, general condition and location of the property.

The Valuation Office no longer changes RVs and water companies are not allowed to change them or use council tax bandings as an alternative.

Find out more at unitedutilities.com/rv

Free Meter Option?
You can choose to have a free meter fitted and be charged for the water you use rather than based on the RV of your home. If you live alone, have a small family or a high RV, you might save money. If it's not for you, you can change back to RV charges if you ask within 13 months of the meter being fitted.

Find out more at **unitedutilities.com/meters** or call us on **0845 746 1100**.

Your account number
417 711 5394

Bill date
10 March 2014

Summary

Amount due on last bill ▶ sent on 11 Mar 13	£389.71
New charges ▶ see below	£401.13
Payments received up to 13 Jan 14 ▶ see page 2	£389.71
Total charges this year	£401.13

Amount now due for your first instalment — £100.29

New charges from 1 April 2014 to 31 March 2015

Water
Standing charge		£63.00
Rateable value charge	Your home's rateable value of £136 multiplied by the £0.983 usage rate	£133.69
2014 Special Discount		£2.50 credit
Total Water charges		£194.19

Wastewater
Rateable value charge	Your home's rateable value of £136 multiplied by the £1.540 usage rate	£209.44
2014 Special Discount		£2.50 credit
Total Wastewater charges		£206.94

Total charges this year 1 Apr 14 to 31 Mar 15 — £401.13

9. THE ENVIRONMENT

Now I turn to the David Bellamy Conservation Awards. Although I'm sure all caravan and park residents are au fait with these annual awards, for the benefit of the reader, I'll quote the 2014 Holiday Parks Guide as follows:

"Parks entering for a David Bellamy Conservation Award are independently audited by a local wildlife body and awarded an accolade (at bronze, silver or gold level) only if they can demonstrate a proven commitment to the highest standards of conservation practice. As well as initiatives such as creating wildlife habitats and planting trees, assessors of the David Bellamy Awards look at all aspects of a park's policies – from recycling to energy efficiency and measures to minimise its carbon footprint"

I am reliably informed that when the assessors visited the park one of them brought along a dog. This dog was allowed to roam free at will. The local paper regularly gives generous coverage to the activities of Pure Leisure Group Ltd. and Fell End Caravan Park.

Confirmation of this can be seen in the numerous cuttings I have on file, one of these measuring 16cm by 17cm provides coverage regarding the 2013 David Bellamy Conservation Awards to Fell End Caravan Park, who received the ultimate accolade – that of Gold status. This award was endorsed and presented by the mayor of Lancaster. During this year, further awards in respect of the "National Quality in Tourism Assessments" (whatever that means!) were presented to Fell End Park by a leading politician, who was also present at the opening of Fell End's new multi-million pound leisure complex in 2010.

During my stay on Fell End Caravan Park (2005-2011) I couldn't help but notice year in and year out a general deterioration of even initial moderate standards regarding the environmental health and safety aspects. My very first concern, small as it may be, was highlighted by the condition of the tree bird boxes. Apart from there being a ridiculously meagre amount throughout the Park's woodland, each and every one of them was totally unfit for purpose, having been ravaged by predators – presumably in their aim to devour the bird's eggs or fledglings. These now defunct bird boxes have remained eye-sores for several years and, what I would have thought, an embarrassment to the park management.

In the early years of my residency I used to enjoy being regularly visited by a peacock, a Lady Amhersts pheasant, several Jays and a pair of French (red-legged) partridges. The French connection each and every year proudly strutted out on a daily basis to show off their new brood of some twelve chicks. They are now all but gone. Today, there is a scarcity of pheasants, once in abundance. This sad situation has been confirmed by an ex-neighbour of mine who still resides on the park.

You will have no doubt realised that in the compilation of my non-fiction book I have deliberately made sure that since I 'left' the park in 2011 contact has been maintained with several current park residents. They have quite willingly provided me with "goings-on" at the park which are, they hope, book material. Moles, you might say.

There is one long serving employee of the park however who, during chats when we occasionally and literally cross paths, has quite innocently revealed information which helps to identify some of the reasons for the park's apathetic approach to its environmental responsibilities culminating in the resultant state of affairs. This person (who I understand has since left his park employers) stated in late 2013 the following, and I quote:

"There is no control whatsoever over the park. Dogs run free and there is no (park) supervision of kids, some of whom run wild without parental control both on the park and in the woodland areas. On occasions they cause damage, a recent example being the application of graffiti on some trees. Even the bats have buggered off"

He was in fact referring to a colony which had hung about one of the park's outbuildings for many years. Further resident feedbacks tell of the continued post-midnight loud music from both the park's leisure complex and certain resident's caravans. We were blessed with the nocturnal presence in our vicinity of a pair of tawny owls. I now wonder at these times if they found it difficult to maintain their senses whilst out hunting. Park rule 9.9 states: "Noise levels must be kept to a minimum after 10.00pm". This must be difficult to maintain when the site manager has long gone home. Home being four miles away.

I read with interest in the April 2014 edition of the park home and holiday caravan magazine, an item concerning a Cumbrian holiday park. The magazine stated the following: "Guests at Skelwith Fold Holiday Park near Ambleside are being sent home with acorns as part of plans to conquer the threat from the disease known as 'sudden oak death'. The park hopes that the acorns will be planted by holiday makers to provide healthy new saplings if the fungus-like invader hits Cumbria". I would also like to add that this park possesses a two-way love relationship with the rare red squirrel. Oh! What a sharp contrast to the Fell End Park where tree planting, the creation of wildlife habitats etc. are unheard of. In early 2014 two healthy, magnificent, tall, mature trees, an oak and a yew, were felled – thus making way for more caravans. I walked under these trees on many an occasion with a feeling of awe which never diminished. It must have taken Mother Nature in harmony with Father Time many, many years to create these two, monumental living things of indescribable beauty. Without these thoughts – only those of greed – they were butchered in a matter of hours.

10. THE "ON AND OFF ASAP" POLICY?

During the time I resided on the Fell End Caravan Park, the occupancy "change-over" within a two hundred yard radius from us was, I would estimate, in excess of fifty percent. What occurred in areas further afield i.e. the rest of the park, apart from a few incidents, I have no direct factual knowledge of – suffice to say varied disturbing tales surfaced. In every single instance the 'departures' I witnessed were, to put it mildly, clouded in sadness. I will later go into detail surrounding ten of these and indeed the financial losses incurred by the residents. Fell End Park's management believe its rules and regulations are impregnable, and are totally enforceable in law. Armed with this (false) belief they are used mercilessly to their advantage whenever they think necessary.

It appears to me that Fell End's disguised aim is to turn over as many sales as possible *per each unit* on their park, thus of course multiplying ongoing profits – even if it means forcing people out of their homes. All this is happening from only one initial capital outlay to the manufacturer, an outlay which generally attracts a universal discount of thirty seven and a half percent. Not one resident ever disclosed to me a discount had been given when purchasing without a trade-in, his new unit. As in my case, nil percent. However with the sales patter of "investment" – "economical way of living" etc. ringing in your ears I, wearing my rose-coloured glasses, plunged like a true sucker into what was to become a catastrophic situation.

Any motor dealers reading this might be forgiven into thinking they are in the wrong business. They usually have to be content with one bite of the cherry, i.e. a profit only on the car they sell, as invariably they 'trade-away' the part exchange. Being involved in a discount is recognised in the motor trade *and* by the public as par for the course. Not, it seems, by the Fell End sales team.

My limited knowledge of actual sales and buy-backs is restricted to ten transactions. I will eventually provide you with as much detail on each as I can. You will of course realise my direct involvement is but a drop in the ocean compared to the overall total of 'deals' completed during Fell End's twenty (plus) year history to date. In three of the 'sales and buy-backs' the victims have allowed me to disclose their names. *My* bitter experience is chronicled in the chapter headed "The Eviction". You will observe that in respect of two of the couples who have agreed to 'go public' I have undisputable and totally damning written evidence of financial malpractice – this, I believe, is tantamount to fraud. But compared with what is to come later in the book this is miniscule. To my mind these available facts provide barometrical evidence in respect of how other Fell End transactions could have taken place of which, may I suggest, there will be hundreds.

11. REVENUES AND OVERHEADS

Whilst reading national caravan magazines etc. I found the common denominator in respect of park caravan site commissions throughout the United Kingdom to be the traditional ten percent. Not so with Fell End Park. Their ruling number 4.11 states: "…pay to the seller of the holiday home the balance due after deducting fifteen percent commission plus V.A.T…." As you know, estate agents normally charge up to two percent in respect of the housing market. This exorbitant commission represents a significant loss of hard-earned equity to the caravan/holiday home owner. It also means that Fell End Park benefits from improvements the resident has made to it. Apart from a little on-park advertising, i.e. photograph on noticeboard, Fell End do nothing else to help the sale. Surely commission in all these instances cannot apply because a commission can only be paid for a job well done or service provided.

Upon scrutinising the official lay-out of the park (Ref. A herein), I note there are the following:
1. Static Caravan plots – 262
2. Touring Caravan plots – 77
3. Pod Camping plots – 9

In respect of static caravans only:

The current 2015 site fees (excluding V.A.T.) charged by Fell End Caravan Park are £2,595.22 per unit. The rates charged are £244.01 per unit (Ref. B herein).

The current rates payable by Fell End to South Lakeland District Council (Ref. C herein) are £53,020. It is interesting to note that the rates payable in 2013 were £54,960 – 3.5% more than the present amount (Ref. D herein).

With regard to the rates, the proven figures demonstrate an income of £63,930.62, i.e. 262 x £244.01 providing the park, so it seems, with a surplus of £10,910.62.

Turning now to the site fees, the proven figures indicate a gross income of £679,947.06 (six hundred and seventy nine thousand, nine hundred and forty seven pounds and sixty six pence). These figures are calculated on the basis that all the static caravan plots are paying their rates and site fees, i.e. occupied. This appears to be the case as indicated by the lay out.

All incomes generated by touring caravans and pods are *not* included. The former's all year round site fees are not much cheaper than static caravans.

In defence of these revenue amounts we must not forget the park's upkeep costs. During my stay on the park its "non-income producing" salaried management consisted of the following:
1. The site manager
2. The site manager's wife
3. Maintenance and park improvement manager
4. Handyman
5. Jobbing gardener
6. Clerical costs (e.g. invoices)

The costs of electric and gas were accounted for and water was free due to the convenience of an on-site natural borehole. The leisure complex and shop were no doubt self-supporting and indeed providing a profit, thus giving a healthy return on the park's £2+ million initial investment – site fees apart!

Reference A

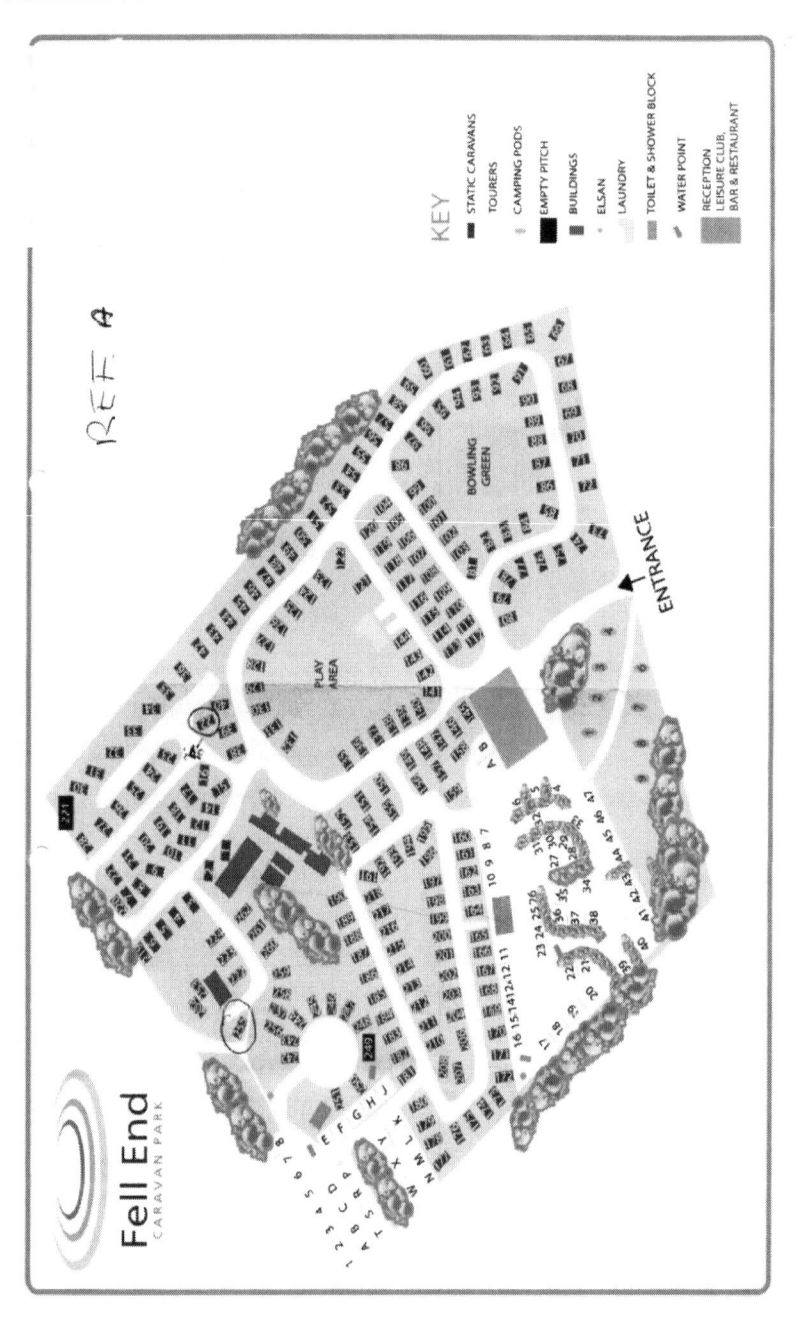

Reference B

Pure Leisure
South Lakeland House
A6 Yealand Redmayne
Carnforth
Lancs
LA5 9RN

Telephone   01524 781918
Fax   01524 782243
VAT Number 514 3195 67

pure leisure

REF B

Invoice

Date   01/11/2014

Account No.

Quantity	Product Description	Unit Price	Net Amount	VAT Amount
1.00	Site Fees for Season 2015/16	2,595.2200	2,595.22	519.04
1.00	Rates for Season	244.0100	244.01	48.80

PLEASE SEND PAYMENTS TO:-

Pure Leisure
Fellend Caravan Park
Slackhead Road
Hale
Milnthorpe
LA7 7BS
Telephone: 015395 62122

Net Amount   2,839.23
VAT Amount   567.84
Invoice Total   3,407.07

Please make cheques payable to
Pure Leisure

Reference C

REF. C

South Lakeland District Council
South Lakeland House
Lowther Street
Kendal
Cumbria
LA9 4DQ

Tel: 01539 733333
www.southlakeland.gov.uk

Mr AS Cooper
1, St. Anthony's Close
Milnthorpe
Cumbria
LA7 7DT

Our Ref: F15023   Your Ref: Date: 14 January 2015

Dear Mr Cooper

FREEDOM OF INFORMATION REQUEST

I am writing in respect of your recent enquiry, dated 11 January 2015, for information held by the Council under the provisions of the Freedom of Information Act. You asked the following:

> Would you kindly advise me of the current rateable value of Fell End Caravan Park and also the business rates payable? Would you also kindly advise me of the amount of rateable value attributable to those caravans (together with their pitches). I would also request the number of caravans occupied by persons upon which your figures can be calculated.

I can confirm the following:

The rateable value of Fell End Caravan Site is £110,000 and the amount payable for the current financial year is £53,020. South Lakeland District Council does not set the rateable value. That is done by the Valuation Office Agency. South Lakeland District Council calculates the amount payable from the rateable value in the Rating List.

If you have any queries, concerns or if you are dissatisfied with the handling of your request please contact me as detailed. Alternatively, if you wish to make an official complaint then please use the Council's complaints procedure, details of which will be provided on request. If you are not content with the outcome of your corporate complaint, you may apply directly to the Information Commissioner.

Further information is available from the Information Commissioner at: Information Commissioner's Office, Wycliffe House, Water Lane, Wilmslow, Cheshire, SK9 5AF.
www.informationcommissioner.gov.uk

Yours sincerely,

Paul Mountford | Principal Performance & Intelligence Officer

Reference D

South Lakeland District Council
South Lakeland House
Lowther Street
Kendal
Cumbria
LA9 4DQ

Tel: 01539 733333
www.southlakeland.gov.uk

Mr S Cooper
1, St. Anthony's Close
Milnthorpe
Cumbria
LA7 7DT

Our Ref: F/102013/3115498   Your Ref: Date: 1 November 2013

Dear Mr Cooper

FREEDOM OF INFORMATION REQUEST - F/102013/3115498

I am writing in respect of your recent enquiry, dated 24 October 2013, for information held by the Council under the provisions of the Freedom of Information Act. You asked the following:

> Advise me the rates payable by the Pure Leisure Group Ltd. In respect of their Caravan Park at fell End, Slackhead Road, Hale, Milnthorpe, LA7 7BS in 2012/13.

I can confirm the following:

The rateable value of Fell End Caravan Park is £120,000 and the Business Rates payable in 2012/13 total £54,960.00.

For further information the amount payable at present for 2013/14 is £56,520.00.

If you have any queries, concerns or if you are dissatisfied with the handling of your request please contact me as detailed. Alternatively, if you wish to make an official complaint then please use the Council's complaints procedure, details of which will be provided on request. If you are not content with the outcome of your corporate complaint, you may apply directly to the Information Commissioner.

Further information is available from the Information Commissioner at: Information Commissioner's Office, Wycliffe House, Water Lane, Wilmslow, Cheshire, SK9 5AF.
www.informationcommissioner.gov.uk

Yours sincerely,

Paul Mountford | Principal Performance & Intelligence Officer

12. CUSTOMER RELATIONS

In time I came to realise that when any of the Pure Leisure's management looked at you (usually off-centre) they didn't see your eyes; only two one pound coins. In other words they had no consideration whatsoever as to your enjoyment, well-being and comfort.

Not on any occasion did I, or any of my fellow residents known to me, receive either a verbal or written communication of a social intercourse nature.

The whole park suffered a totally unacceptable amount of malfunctions occurring on a regular basis throughout the years of my residence. I am led to believe that this situation is still ongoing (see elsewhere in the book).

To be fair, however, I do recall an instance when a notice was affixed to the main doors of the leisure complex advising that the electric was to be cut off between the hours of 10am and 2pm. Intimation of any regret did not accompany the statement. We had no electricity for eight hours.

I'll give you ten examples regarding the virtual non-existence on the art of customer relations although I, and many others I'm sure, could recount a great deal more.

1. At the (grand?) official opening of the new Fell End multi-million pound leisure complex from beginning to end the dignitaries ate and drank alone, aloof and far apart from a good turn-out of the park's residents. They looked curiously on at the so-called top brass who eventually departed and, just as they had arrived, went without a single word, smile or nod to those who in effect had made the occasion possible. It was later remarked by one of the 'lookers-on' that "it all made me feel like a plebeian" – although in rather stronger phraseology.
2. For six weeks of the year, residents were only allowed to be

present in their homes from 10am to 4pm, i.e. no overnight stay. This ruling applied to the period from 16th January to 28th February. On our first ever enforced departure we were in the process of leaving when a loud knocking took place outside the door. It turned out to be the park manager, who demanded that we leave that very instant. I automatically checked my watch which showed the time to be 4:02pm.

3. After two years in residence I believed a pretty good relationship had developed with those all around us. I still had grave doubts however, not only as to the Pure Leisure Group H.Q. management, but more locally - the Fell End Park controllers, particularly the manager. Continuing the theme on public relations, a Mr. Alan Green wrote to me whilst we were in the middle of our six week break from the park. At the time he held the title of communications director, based at Pure Leisure's headquarters. According to his letter the park manager had asked him to look at the area of land surrounding our holiday home, pointing out "the erection of a large shed, the removal of shrubs owned by the park, removal of top soil and gravel revealing the telephone cables and other services. Will you re-instate the works to their previous state and apply to Mr. Proudfoot for permission to be carried out in respect to any further alterations to the pitch and its surroundings". I will write no more on this save to say it is the subject of my pen at a later stage, and that the manager's house is adjacent to the manager's office, which is no more than a distance of one hundred yards from our home.

4. We were graced in our little Thwaite by the presence of two wonderful neighbours, Alan and Edie. Their marriage was in its 50th year when we arrived. You couldn't meet a nicer and happier couple. They had moved to Fell End six years previously to enjoy their retirement. They made sure we were more than welcome and in no time invited us across for a 'get-to-know-you' evening meal. It was superb, although the Bury tradition of cheese with fruit cake took a bit of swallowing.

Edie was the life and soul of our community, and became well-known to the park's management, calling every day without fail to collect her mail, papers, groceries etc.

One dark, wet November night Edie died suddenly. I called the emergency services with full details and duly waited for the paramedics. In respect of the vital final directions and name details the resultant first responder was somehow misinformed by the Park's office. This resulted in him calling at *our* holiday residence. Ironically and coincidentally he was an ex-park resident and a good friend of ours. Outside in the pouring rain he came up close, looked at me with a mixture of apprehension and sadness and said: "Is it Margaret?"

My main theme in this story of Edie's demise was the fact that Alan in time pointed out to me that he was disappointed in not having received any condolences whatsoever from the park management, both at the time and in the weeks that followed. A couple of years later he did receive a telephone call demanding payment of his site fee deposit which he had in fact paid on time, as Edie had done so every day since their arrival.

5. A friend and fellow park resident of mine who lives in Bourneville, Birmingham, had been away from the park all day, over the hills of the Lake District, whilst his son had been attempting to contact him urgently due to an emergency at home. There being no mobile telephone signal he contacted Fell End and explaining the situation and requesting them to contact his father immediately upon his return to the park – or at least leave a message at his caravan. He was advised that it was not company policy to take any action (pass on) regarding messages of a third party nature. Later, after dark, a distraught son managed to speak with his seventy-seven year old dad who immediately sped down the motorway filled with thoughts of anxiety and needless to say, anger. I have no wish to elongate on the eventual outcome surrounding my friend and his family however suffice to say the park's rule number 13.3 states: "telephone messages will not be taken by the park office except in an emergency".

6. Whilst cleaning out our new caravan's gutters for the first time, I noticed a serious dint in the apex of the roof. The park management said they would look into it. My several requests of action from the park were ignored. I eventually obtained an estimate of repair from a very well-respected company (who turned out to be on the insurer's approved list) and sent it off. Of the many questions asked on the claim form I had to answer

"don't know" to almost all of them. To my surprise they accepted the claim without query. The repairs were then duly carried out and paid for, the sum being £265.00, and my no claims discount went out the window. Or should I say roof? When I approached the park management regarding reimbursement, I was given a look of incredulity as if to say, had I gone out of my mind?

7. For some years the park's management allowed residents to advertise miscellaneous items in their shop window. There was no charge for this service, only a suggested voluntary payment. These contributions helped fund the children's annual Christmas party. The owner of Fell End, upon espying the small card adverts, ordered them to be removed, stating: "I give enough to charity".

8. Almost touching the rear of our caravan were several large boulders firmly embedded in the ground. This meant we could not clean the back of the caravan, and indeed the windows. Neither could we walk around it (my wife actually injured herself on these stones). All efforts to get the park to move them failed. As part of my 'jungle to garden' aim however, and with the help of three neighbours, a land rover and a chain we managed to move these obstructions. We took advantage of the situation and lined the boulders up to form a perfect natural boundary to the garden which ran alongside a woodland footpath, killing two birds with more than one stone, so to speak. However the park then decided their mobile shoveller/digger could in future take a short-cut using the footpath, the snag being that at the point where my boulders were now in place and, although they were within my boundary lines, they were adjacent to a bend. This meant that at this point the machine could not manoeuvre to get through. My boundary of stones was bulldozed out of the way, ruining part of the garden together with the relatively new shrubs and plants therein. Adopting a philosophical attitude I mused that at least I had finally got the park to move the boulders.

9. On a similar theme some time later my caravan was chipped whilst the park were laying new T.V. cables. As with the roof and boulders scenario they admitted nothing.

An elderly couple, whom I will call Mr. and Mrs. B, came to

reside on the park. On my daily travels I had to pass by their home. This resulted in us exchanging pleasantries almost on a weekly basis.

It became apparent to me that they were reserved, even shy folk. Wishing for a quiet and peaceful retirement I respected this situation, and didn't over-indulge in extended conversations. We just passed the time of day.

In time I couldn't help but observe they kept at all times an immaculately clean both car and caravan, together with the creation of a small but beautiful garden. They, I was pleased to believe, were happy.

A year or so after their arrival, I was mildly surprised on passing by to hear "Mr. Cooper, have you a minute?" It was Mrs. B., who then asked me into their home. In the interests of neighbourly relations I happily accepted, only to be confronted with an atmosphere of gloom and despondency. In addition I found Mr. B. also distraught. They then explained to me the reason for their demeanour.

Their garden was adjacent to work being carried out as part of the park's new, underground electrical cabling system. Without any warning whatsoever, in short-cutting the trenching line, the park's workmen dug across the garden, destroying anything in its resultant path. This work was carried out by Fell End Park staff, led by one of the Morphet family, namely Matthew, known as Matt.

Taking pride of place in the garden, a small grey headstone had been erected in memory of Mrs. B.'s father. It was inscribed with a few poignant words.

After a futile attempt to console the couple, I departed, but not before Mrs B. took me to the hedge at the back of the garden. This was away from where the excavating took place. There, under the hedge, lay the headstone. Neither of them had the courage to rescue it. This desecration was the real reason for my visit. I was proud in renovating and re-erecting to the best of my ability their treasured memory. I was also sad and angry.

From thereon in I made regular visits during which time Mr. B. disclosed his wife had multiple sclerosis, the main reason for choosing the holiday home lifestyle. Then one day, without a word to anyone, they were gone.

INTERLUDE – PAUSE FOR THOUGHT

Did Fate's path guide me to write this book? Perhaps arriving at Fell End was not my chosen desire for a reclusive woodland (caravan) life after all. Or was it a mission unbeknown to me for this park's corruption to be revealed at last? I do not wish to appear grandiose in any shape or form but was I "the chosen one"? Nonetheless this 'fantasy thought' helped drive me on in the compilation and completion of this book. Perhaps you may or may not understand but support has also emanated as follows: During my writings (and again without seeming overdramatic) I kept recalling the following words, which are amongst the most famous words in English literature, the start of which reads: "It is a far, far greater thing I have done now than I have ever done". I don't think I have to remind you that the book "a Tale of Two Cities" by Charles Dickens takes the credit. I bet his book took less effort than this one: the difference I suppose lies in the word genius. Notwithstanding the forgoing my efforts could, I hope, help kick-start its own type of revolution.

13. THE SALES AND BUY-BACKS SECTION I

In the ten instances I am about to disclose, only one resident removed his holiday home. All the others, including myself (I had no choice in the matter) succumbed to the park's buy-back offer – this is not as surprising as it may sound. The following points, I hope, will give you a better understanding.
1. For whatever reason you have become filled with (understandable) disillusionment. You just want out, as quickly as possible, without fuss. Then you finally become deflated, and shocked at the buy-back offer.
2. Where would you find a suitable place to site your 38ft. by 12ft. static caravan? The front garden?
3. Overnight your caravan has become a symbol of annoyance, a handicap, a financial disaster, (is this the main reason?) an embarrassment, a burden.
4. Park ruling 4.12 – an abbreviation – states: "any owner who wishes to remove a holiday home from the park… a reasonable charge will be made for disconnection…".

Prior to my 2011 departure, the charge including V.A.T. was the neck end of £1,000. A reasonable estimate would show a maximum of one hours labour without any capital outlay. Incidentally up until the season of 2013 no matter when you decided to quit, whether it be after one month or more, no refund of site fees applied. Even today, after six months residency refunds are zeroed. More of this later.

Each and every one of the sale and buy-back transactions were orchestrated by a Pure Leisure Group employee, namely a certain Mr. Andrew Crowe of their sales division. You will observe his name cropping up on a regular basis. I have reserved a chapter for my analysis of him to be read later in the book. In digesting these transactions I'm sure you will fully understand why he deserves a

special mention.
1. Michael
2. 'Helen' and 'Howard' – their real names I have changed as they would have wished.
3. Neil and Christine
4. Phil and Moira
5. 'Plot 173'

Note: I have left Section two until after my revelations about "The Crowe on the Park". This, if needed, will give you time to step back and take in the contents of Section one. Also, parts of section two are even more mind-boggling than its forgoer.

1. Michael

Michael was enforced to leave the park due to illness. He went to live in a flat in Kendal, a town about ten miles away. This is where, a year or so after his departure, by chance I met up with him. He looked dreadful. Not having had the opportunity prior to now, he 'opened up' and told me of his leaving the park was due to health reasons – cancer. This also meant being near to his Kendal-based daughter. In the course of our chat he told me that he had paid £30,000.00 (thirty thousand pounds) for his park home. On leaving the park some two years later he received £2,000.00 (two thousand pounds) for same.

Listening to his frail protestations at the park's offer he was advised the caravan at the time of his purchase was *not* new, as he was lead to believe. They further explained to him that whilst he was the first owner, the unit had been in storage (awaiting sale?) for two years. Michael was a calm, lovely man, still very much affected by a tragedy of some years ago.

You will appreciate that, whilst he once owned a thriving fish merchant's business, he had become extremely vulnerable to anyone wishing to take advantage of his condition. Not long after our tête-à-tête he passed away.

2. "Helen and Howard"

Helen and Howard came to live on the park but had gone within eighteen months. When living in a caravan on a permanent basis you will appreciate it's capable for catering for no more than two people. This soon became obvious to these proud parents of their fast growing-up son. No-one to blame, a quite understandable situation created due to inexperience of this home life-style. Our son came to live temporarily with us – we know. So they quite innocently placed a for-sale sign in their window.

In the eyes of Fell End Park, this action seriously contravened their rules and regulations. The only rules at the time which could be in any way associated with their action are rules 4.1 to 4.9, later becoming 4.1 to 4.13. These, in effect, stated that you must first offer the home to the company. If they don't wish to purchase, permission to sell must be in writing from them: conducted through their office as your agents, who will deduct 15% (not 10%) off the balance due to the seller of the holiday home – in this case H.&H.

So, therefore, in a matter of hours whilst her husband was at work, Helen was visited upon by Mr. Crowe. Her son was present. She recounted to me in detail Mr Crowe's verbal, high-pitched, frenzied threats, one of these being the removal of their home from the park before midnight. Upon my gentle insistence she quoted ad-lib the majority of the contents of Mr Crowe's diatribe. What had spat from his mouth I find unfit for publication in this book.

Helen never recovered from Mr. Crowe's onslaught, and this accelerated their departure with the usual buy-back transaction taking place. A very saleable unit now quickly on the market at probably three times the buy-back figure, which was £10,000.00 (ten thousand pounds). Mr Crowe's mission accomplished.

Totally irrelevant to this book's cause, but you may be interested to know that this couple, six years later, have bought their own house. They are both involved in medical health care at a local hospital where Mr. Crowe was subsequently fined for parking in an area reserved for staff.

We have remained friends to this day, and meet up every so often. Neither Helen nor Howard ever discuss their Fell End Park experience.

3. Neil and Christine

Not quite a sale and buy-back – far from it in fact. Christine and Neil, a couple from Yorkshire, visited the park most weekends (they were not 'full-timers'). They purchased their holiday home from Fell End via Mr. Crowe for £12,000 (twelve thousand pounds).

Genuine, pleasant people who made excellent neighbours, they obviously enjoyed the park way of life, especially in our woodland environment. Neil, I observed, was a carpenter extraordinaire possessing the sight in one eye only. With his skills he changed his basic unit to one that you could only but admire. The finished article, for example, included double glazed units (replacing P.V.C. singular windows throughout), finished with dark wood surrounds. New strengthened flooring was installed together with central heating and detached furnishings replacing the bench-type seating which was flush with the walls and immovable. I witnessed the creation of these dramatic improvements, as did my wife Margaret, who knows how I struggle in changing a fuse.

Mr Crowe duly visited them, as a result of which:
1. They were ordered off the park, together with their caravan.
2. "Because the caravan has been de-standardized I cannot offer even one penny for it". They were stunned.

We returned to the park after having been away for a few days to find, apart from the metal garden shed, an empty plot. Christine and Neil were keen gardeners. They had transformed a scrub into a lovely garden. They had left all items connected with their garden's upkeep and maintenance with me, together with a note, part of which read: "Sep, don't let the vultures get the shed". And did they?

Christine and Neil were our friends and neighbours for about two years. I later discovered they had made their own removal arrangements. The park did not receive their disconnection fee. I leave you to guess if Mr. Crowe had ulterior motives as to his dastardly and draconian attitude. If so, what were they? Let us not forget Christine and Neil's small caravan was sited on an outstanding plot, one which was deserving of and being graced by a top range model. And so it came to pass. We have not seen or heard from Christine and Neil ever since. I do not in the slightest way find this surprising. I believe they wish to obliterate their memory of the park, the ending of which far and away smothered all their happy times.

4. Phil and Moira

This sale and buy-back involves a log cabin. It is situated across from our (humble in comparison) caravan. As I write this factual account I breathe sighs of relief I didn't purchase this type of holiday home. As the pages unfold you will realise why.

Phil and Moira, Liverpudlians in the construction industry, were on the park four or so years ago before our arrival in 2005. Although not full-timers, they and their family spent a good deal of their social hours here.

I was disappointed when Phil told me he had to sell his cabin due to ever increasing business commitments, and thus be more 'on hand' at the works. We'd had a very good neighbourly relationship. When he finally departed he gave me two magnificent bamboo plants which stood proudly in their beautiful, expensive ceramic pots. It was obvious they had spent a great deal of time etc. in improving the cabin's outward appearance, which included decking all round, finished off with an impressive built-up patio and striking illuminations. No doubt the cabin's interior has received similar treatment. I thought it would be courteous not to collect the plants until after they had departed.

Phil put up a for sale sign both inside his window and at the park entrance, much to the chagrin of Mr. Crowe. A few days later the sign inside the cabin was removed as I observed Mr. Crowe leaping up and grabbing hold of the patio's balustrade. He then clambered over, opened the French windows and disappeared inside for a good five minutes. Later that day I 'borrowed' my spare set of keys from the Park's office. Permanently.

Phil and Moira had paid £75,000 (seventy five thousand pounds) for the (basic) cabin. No discount being entertained. Seven years later, the buy-back transaction yielded them £17,000 (seventeen thousand pounds). The cabin was then sold for £55,000 (fifty five thousand pounds). A loss to Phil and Moira of £58,000 (fifty eight thousand pounds), not forgetting the thousands they had spent on it. This equates to £8,285 per annum i.e. £159 per week (which I know you will have already worked out!).

All these figures have been confirmed to me by Eric, the park manager at the time, and by the new purchasers, Barbara and Steve.

When one gives it thought, the moving of a large log cabin would require a great deal of expertise, coupled with a lot of man and machine power. Far easier to sell it back (on site) and be done with it.

Early morning on the day after my neighbours' departure from the park (never to return), two park employees scaled the log cabin's decking and with the aid of a motor and trailer they quickly departed with their booty – the beautiful bamboo plants! I then quickly readied myself for the day and sought out the person responsible for this theft; Mr. Matt Morphet.

I explained the situation and in requesting the return of the plants I was abruptly informed they were included in the buy-back price of the cabin by Fell End. I realised there and then the door had been shut firmly in my face.

I became aware of the plants' new home and over time watched them, due to a total lack of care, slowly die.

Plot Number 173

One of my resident moles, who has now recently left the park, lived for a good number of years (a full-timer) very near to the above plot. He knew all the different owners personally. He kept, for reasons of his own, a sale and buy-back account of all the transactions concerning the caravan sited at this plot. They are as follows:

The Caravan Incomes:
A. Initial sale proceeds: £30,000
B. Second sale proceeds: £25,000
C. Third sale proceeds: £16,000
D. Disconnection fee: £750
Total: £71,750

Cost of the Caravan Purchases:
A. Net of manufacturer's discount (37.5%): £18,750
B. First buy-back: £2,000
C. Second buy-back: £8,000
Total: £28,750

Net profit to Fell End Caravan Park: £43,000

On a similar theme as to what took place with sale and buy-back number four (Phil and Moira), I relate the following:

In 2005 Fell End Park's welcoming brochure stated: "If you are a new customer and want to order a wooden skirting when buying your caravan, we can offer this service from just £350.00 including V.A.T.". Three years later, after my son-in-law had completed the construction of a magnificent, large balcony and all-round skirting for £1,000, I was left with a considerable amount of 3" x 2" treated wooden lengths. These, upon my permanently leaving the park, I left in the temporary and safe care of a kind neighbour and friend,

Alan. In due course I forewarned Alan that the wood was to be collected. On the morning of the agreed day of collection he kindly stacked the wood out in the open, thus facilitating easy removal. He pointed out, however, that he would not be on site at the time of the collection. I had made no charge for the wood, which was just as well. It had gone. To this day the potential beneficiary doesn't believe my explanation as to why I sent him on a six mile wild goose chase. I regularly see him in the village of Milnthorpe, where I now live. He still shakes his head, although a wry smile does come with it.

14. A CROWE ON THE PARK

"Nobody on this park has a legal leg to stand on". This bold (anti-sales?) statement, was put to me very early on during my stay at Fell End, by the head of caravan sales. Mr. A. Crowe. In truth it sounded like a disguised warning. Whatever, it set the tone in respect of my attitude towards him throughout my stay on the park. Needless to say, my awareness of a few of the ongoing 'sale and buy-back' scenarios deepened my alienation towards him. He was permanently oblivious to this. I was always on edge when he was around. I kept thinking, is it the sensitivity in my make-up or the total lack of it in his? In time I came to realise it was without a doubt the latter.

Eventually it became obvious that Mr. Crowe was, and is to this day, in total control of all aspects to do with sales and buy-backs. In his belief, he ruled the roost. He has a free rein, the park's principle pillager plundering holiday home-owners' savings and then their assets at will. This soulless person obviously has the full backing of Fell End Park's owner. No – *not* the Pure Leisure Group Ltd. but "Pure Leisure, which refers to the sole trader business of Mr. J. C. Morphet, the sole owner of the park. The Pure Leisure office is at South Lakeland House, A6, Yealand Redmayne, Carnforth, Lancs, LA5 9RN". I quote from the Fell End Park's site licence and site rules to be found under "introduction and summary". (I hope to disclose more of this conundrum later in the book). South Lakeland House incidentally, is in Lancashire. Another oddity.

I cannot help but liken Mr. Crowe to 'a poor man's' Harlen Maguire, a hired assassin played by Jude Law in the film "Road to Perdition". With haste I totally and unreservedly apologise to Mr. Law and trust if he is made aware of (or indeed reads) this book he will appreciate the context in which it is written.

It was well known in local circles Mr. Crowe imbibed prodigiously when it came to alcohol; so much so that he once fell off a table at the Pure Leisure Group's annual ball. He was subsequently relieved (sacked) from his duties but was later reinstated. It is thought that he is now a teetotaller.

The crow belongs to the magpie family. It is attracted to articles which sparkle and shine, such as a vacuum pack when under the glare of a shop's display lights. This, the crow finds irresistible, especially when the pack contains food, e.g. bacon.

Now this particular crow, was espied on no less than three weekly occasions, stealing the described items from the Fell End Park's leisure complex shop. The crow's plan of attack was to hang around (hover), attempting an air of inconspicuousness until the day-time shop assistants left. The security shutters remained in the 'open' position because the shop then became the responsibility of the bar staff, based up to ten metres away. They could at times, be understandably occupied serving drinks etc.. It was then the crow would swoop.

Putting his ill-gotten gains under his wing, he would then head in a straight line for the main exit doors. As the crow flies, so to speak.

My witnesses to these acts of downright theft reside on the park and regularly drink at the bar overlooking the shop. They are two retired businessmen, of impeccable character, who have confirmed they would testify in a court of law to the truth of their information, disclosed to me in confidence in early 2014. I was disappointed to learn that they have since left the park.

Should court proceedings take place, the crow could be given bird by the beak – yes. I just couldn't resist.

I have noticed that part of Mr. Crowe's high flying sales and marketing campaign during 2014 consists of advertising as follows:
1. Road verge yellow, small, plastic flag signs stuck in the ground bearing an oddly shaped initial 'M' made to resemble 'A.A'. Despite his past weaknesses I do not think his intentions were to lead travellers to the annual alcoholics anonymous conference.
2. Affixing large signs (again in 'A.A. yellow') with the wording "caravan show" to speed limit warning signs, and indeed on a

trunk road, namely the A6.
3. Siting an encapsulated, coloured, illustrated advertisement in a fish and chip shop (no less).
4. Same again on an outside public notice board, amongst the hoped for sales of a miscellaneous nature, e.g. "second hand dishwasher, one owner £15.00", "free rabbit to a good home". I've had my own cards here. Never failed. But really - "Pre-owned holiday homes from £36,000"?
5. There is a one-worded sign outside Fell End Park on the public thoroughfare. It says 'breakfast'. What chance that this meal could eventually turn out to be the most expensive ever eaten? Especially with Crow Caravan Caviar to follow?

15. THE SALES AND BUY-BACKS SECTION II

6. Mick and Sandra
7. Jonathan and Dianne
8. Ken and Sue
9. Bill and Anne
10. Kevin and Sue

Despite gaining only a relatively miniscule amount of 'park knowledge' ten human, sad stories are herein being brought to light. How many more have taken place at the Fell End (holiday) park? Aye, there lies the rub.

6. Mick and Sandra

Mancunians Mick and Sandra Moore have given me authority to reveal all in my book, including their willingness to confirm all you are about to read. Sandra instructs even to "tell the World". Believe it or not this *is* my ultimate goal.

Sandra was a typical Lancashire lass, full of fun with a bubbly, exuberant personality. In contrast, her hubby Mark was the quiet one – he was big, moustachioed and bald. A meek giant. Their very presence provided an uplift in one's company. That was all to change.

Not long after their arrival, the park became understaffed, thus giving Mick and Sandra part-time employment opportunities. To them, this was icing on the cake. Sandra and Mick worked diligently in the park's shop and behind the bar respectively.

As time went by, their caravan became damp from top to bottom, so much so that the wall to wall carpeting became rotten. After several requests, Mr. Crowe turned up and agreed to replace the carpet. Gradually, however, this new carpet began to show signs of excessive damp. Mr. Crowe suggested they put bowls of salt around the caravan. In addition to this state of affairs, and to quote Sandra: "The electric was going off every two minutes". They continued to point out (diplomatically complain) the on-going, ever worsening health hazard, but with no success whatsoever. Hope sprung eternal, however, when they were called into the office, only to find themselves being handed their wages to date. Their top class, popular services evidently were no longer required. No thanks, no explanation, no nothing.

After all this, Sandra was found sobbing on the park by David Griffiths, the park's handyman. She explained to him the reasons for her anguish, these being that she and Mick believed they were going to a better way of (country) life. They had pooled their life savings, most of which had been spent on purchasing the caravan, the price of this being £27,000 (twenty seven thousand pounds). Their marriage of twenty nine years was in danger of breaking up. Sandra has even reached the stage where she had given Mick and ultimatum, "I'm going back to Manchester with or without you". They, of course, duly left together after two years on the park.

With the proceeds of the buy-back transaction £10,000 (ten thousand pounds) in the bank, they then, wisely or not, made discreet but positive enquiries as to the price required to purchase their past home. It had in fact, they were informed, been sold for £28,000 (twenty eight thousand pounds).

7. Jonathan and Dianne

Jonathan and Dianne purchased in 2010 what is known as a park home. Because of its width it has to be transported in two split sections. Almost immediately after taking residence the park had to 'put them up' in a hotel. This was due to serious problems with the new home's floor. Two to three weeks later they were able to return.

After three years on the park they decided to leave. In a buy-back transaction they received the sum of £40,000 (forty thousand pounds). Three years earlier they had paid £100,000 (one hundred thousand pounds) for the same unit. I have it on good authority that at the time of the buy-back Mr. Crowe denied the park home was sold as new and that they were specifically informed it was five years old.

Dianne had occasion to call at my home in March 2014 and confirmed the aforementioned figures, admitting the Fell End experience had cost her £60,000 (sixty thousand pounds). Or, as us laymen would figure it out, £385.00 (three hundred and eighty five pounds) per week. Very surprisingly she refused to make any further comment on the subject and indeed refused my offer to investigate.

I cannot confirm or prove the information disclosed to me by a highly respected current resident of Fell End Park, which was that the park home in question was quickly resold for £90,000 (ninety thousand pounds).

Fell End's dealings in this instance and also in the sale and buy-back number four appear to openly disregard and totally contradict the statements of their associated company, the Pure Leisure Group Ltd.. These are highlighted in extensive press advertisements, among which are stated: "great investment opportunity", and "they are delighted at their purchase and who were considering buying another cabin to rent out to further their investment". Also, "with potentially great returns it's a wonderful way to invest your money".

8. Ken and Sue

Ken and Sue purchased from Fell End a 2008 Willerby Granada on the 8th of December 2011. See receipt for £29,500 (twenty nine thousand, five hundred pounds) of this date which appears to have a number reference 2008-11. This, together with the deposit of £500.00 (five hundred pounds) as shown on the invoice (sale no.) dated the 21st October 2011 gives a total sale price of £30,000 (thirty thousand pounds). In fact, the net sale price figure was £26,834 (twenty six thousand eight hundred and thirty four pounds). Site fees of £3165.50 for the coming 2012 season being "thrown in".

The buy-back transaction yielded just over three years later, in February 2014, the sum of £4,500 (four thousand five hundred pounds).

In the February 2014 edition of Glasses guide to caravan prices, page 463 shows the cost *new* for this caravan to be £23,311 (twenty three thousand three hundred and eleven pounds). My telephone call direct to the manufacturers confirmed this figure, although they would not commit themselves to print without knowing the chassis/serial number. This is nowhere to be seen on Fell End Park's invoice or correspondence. Ever Arthur Daley wouldn't dare omit the equivalent of a serial number, in his case a car's registration (even if it *was* the wrong one).

Sue and Kevin's ex-caravan was quickly back on the market displaying a price tag of £20,000 (twenty thousand pounds). Information received from one of my resident park moles.

Herein you will see copies of the Pure Leisure Group's "Repairs and Renewals" invoices. They, at first site, may not appear significant, however apart from endorsing earlier correspondence on Fell End's invoicing methods, further study shows that it appears they are just 'plucking figures out of thin air' just to suit their needs – take time – have a secondary glance at these three, "one hour labour" invoices. Fell End are prepared to rip you off no matter how small or large the subject involved.

Another example of this is as follows: when a pool table was introduced into the new leisure complex in 2010, the charge was £1.00 per game. Now imagine the following scenario: if you left them with a tin full of roses chocolates and said "help yourselves – I won't be long", we know how many would be there when you returned. The question is – would the tin still be there?

I apologise for getting side-tracked. I let Sue and Ken have a statement of account. A copy is herein. A house, was in fact sold to help finance the caravan.

Finally, I have observed that whenever Fell End Park have a caravan for sale they never show the year of manufacture relating to the same. For example, kindly refer to the enclosed advert. Every single used car sales outlet in this world display the year of the vehicle at every stage of the hoped-for sale. There would be no hope whatsoever if they didn't.

Holiday Homes for sale at two 5* parks situated in the Arnside and Silverdale Area of Outstanding Natural Beauty.

Fantastic Pre Owned Ideal Starter Home
ABI Arizona 28ftx10ft 2 Bed
Enclosed decking on a corner plot, close to children's outdoor play area
Garden shed included!
From £13,995

Exceptional Quality Pre-owned Holiday Home
Pemberton Verona 38ft x 12ft 3 Bed
DG and CH
On a fantastic pitch overlooking one of our greens with an private enclosed garden
From £36,000

Great Value for Money Pre-owned Holiday Home
Cosalt Carlton Super 35ft x 12ft 2 Bed
Includes garden shed!
From £12,500

Exclusive NEW Holiday Home
Pure Escape 37x12 3 Bed
DG and CH—available on a choice of plots
Centre lounge making it the perfect layout for a family holiday home.
From £39,995

Last remaining seasonal touring pitches available at both of the above 5* Parks

To view any of the above holiday homes and for more information

Call Andy on 01524 784784

RECEPTION RECEIPT

2008-11

pure leisure

PARK: HEAD OFFICE
UNIT NUMBER: FE199

BOOKING REF. NO. _____   NO. IN PARTY: _____
GUEST'S NAME: _____   PHONE NUMBER: _____
ADDRESS: 33 PADDOCK WAY
STORTH, CUMBRIA
POSTCODE: _____

PERIOD COMMENCING: _____   FINISH: _____
DEPOSIT: £ _____

Willerby Granada ACCOMMODATION CHARGE: £ _____
36 x 12 2 bed   SURCHARGE: £ _____
2007   TOURER: £ _____
                 INSURANCE: £ _____
                 OTHER: £ 29,500-00

CHANGE OF ACCOMMODATION
FROM: _____   TO: _____

HOW PAID:
CHEQUE / P/O / CASH / GIRO / CREDIT CARD [signature]
DATE: 8/12/4   RECEIVED: [signature]

Please Note: Departure time is 10.00am. All keys & passes must be returned to Reception

CAR REGISTRATION NO: _____

PURE LEISURE GROUP
South Lakeland House, Yealand Redmayne, Carnforth, Lancashire. LA5 9RN.
t: 01524 781918 f: 01524 782243

AUTHOR: "According to this document the transaction took place with the Pure Leisure Group NOT the sole trader business of Pure Leisure T/A Fell End Caravan Park."

Fell End Caravan Park

Slackhead Road, Hale, Milnthorpe, LA7 7BS
Tel: 015395 62122   Fax: 015395 63810

Sale No: RE-WRITE   Sale

PERSONAL DETAILS – "Holiday Home Owner" or "Customer" including permanent address

PLEASE COMPLETE IN BLACK INK & BLOCK CAPITALS

Name: MR KEN WILLIAM SHAW AND SUE BARTON
Address: 33 PADDOCK WAY STORTH CUMBRIA
Postcode: LA7 7JJ   Tel No: 015247627720

HOLIDAY HOME DETAILS

Make: WILLERBY	MODEL: GRANADA	Year: 2008
Size: 36X12	Beds: 2	
Current Location: FB199		
New Location: FE199	Serial/Chassis No:	Stock No: #87

Source of Sale:

		Incl.	To be invoiced
Purchase Price:	£26634.50	Siting & Connection	INC
Site Fees INC FOR 2011	£3163.50 FOR 2012	Rates	INC
Trade in Allowance (subject to cond./year)	(£)		
Deposit:	Cash £500	Steps	INC
	C/Card £	Fridge (new/used)	INC
(Deposits are non-refundable)	Cheque £	Skirting	INC
		Decking	NA
Finance TOTAL TO FINANCE (if applicable)		Gas Bottles – detail no. & size	2X19
Total Balance Due:	£29,500	Gas Regulator/Hose	INC
(Deposits are non-refundable)	Deposit Outstanding £	ADDITIONAL ITEMS TO BE INVOICED – LIST!	
Completion Date: END NOV OR ASAP			

PART EXCHANGE DETAILS

Unit Checked by:		
Make:	Model:	
Size:	Beds:	Pitch
Serial No:	Year:	
Finance Company:	Stock No:	
Settlement Figure: £	Agreement no:	
	Valid To (date):	

Insurance: It is a requirement of your Site Licence that you maintain adequate insurance on your holiday home. This can be arranged by Pure Leisure if required. If you choose to make alternative insurance arrangements you must submit a copy of your Insurance Certificate to the Park Office on completion.

By signing this document you agree to (i) to purchase the Holiday Home on the terms & conditions at the price shown; (ii) that you will not have ownership, tenancy or other proprietary interest in the pitch on which the Holiday Home is sited (iii) to part exchange your Holiday Home which you confirm is your property, free from any hire purchase/conditional sale agreement, charge, lien or third party claim of any kind except as stated on this document.

NOTES/ADDITIONAL ITEMS INCLUDED WITH THE SALE

Fell End Caravan Park is operated as a Holiday Park and your attention is drawn to the fact that holiday homes cannot be occupied during the closed season each year, excepting the details outlined in your copy of the Park Rules. The holiday home may not be used except for holiday or recreational accommodation and there is no right to reside in or use the same as your only or main residence. This is a legally binding agreement which you should only sign if you are satisfied with its terms & conditions. You should understand that the purchase price of the Holiday Home and any resale value are subject to a variety of factors and resale value may reduce or increase over time.

Signature (Customer(s)):

Signed: Date: 22/10/2011
ANDY   & on behalf of Pure Leisure   PRINT NAME: ANDY CROWE

FOR OFFICE USE ONLY

	✓ or X	Holiday Home SIV	£	✓ or X	Part Exchange SIV	£	Finance	£
ON ORIGINAL					Approved By (Park/Sales Manager):			

For PX only – Used Unit Checklist attached   For Referrals – Customer Referral attached

South Lakeland House
A6 Yealand Redmayne
Carnforth
Lancs
LA5 9RN

Telephone   01524 781918
Fax   01524 782243

VAT Number 514 3195 67

Mr K Shaw & Mrs S Barton - FE199
33 Paddock Wa
Storth
Cumbria
LA7 7JJ

Invoice   6147
Date   17/04/2013
Account No. FSHA105
Order No.

Quantity	Product Description	Net Amount	VAT Amount
1.00	Call out to room stat	75.00	15.00

PLEASE SEND PAYMENTS TO:-

Pure Leisure
Fellend Caravan Park
Slackhead Road
Hale
Milnthorpe
LA7 7BS
Telephone: 015395 62122

Net Amount	75.00
VAT Amount	15.00
Invoice Total	90.00

A6 Yealand Redmayne
Carnforth
Lancs
LA5 9RN

Telephone   01524 781918
Fax   01524 782243

VAT Number   514 3195 67

pure leisure

Mr K Shaw & Mrs S Barton - FE199
33 Paddock Wa
Storth
Cumbria
LA7 7JJ

Invoice	6148
Date	17/04/2013
Account No.	FSHA105
Order No.	0882

Quantity	Product Description	Net Amount	VAT Amount
1.00	Repairs to boiler fan - stuck	29.00	5.80

PLEASE SEND PAYMENTS TO:-

Pure Leisure
Fellend Caravan Park
Slackhead Road
Hale
Milnthorpe
LA7 7BS
Telephone: 015395 62122

Net Amount	29.00
VAT Amount	5.80
Invoice Total	34.80

South Lakeland House
A6 Yealand Redmayne
Carnforth
Lancs
LA5 9RN

Telephone 01524 781918
Fax   01524 782243

VAT Number 514 3195 67

pure leisure

Mr K Shaw & Mrs S Barton - FE199
33 Paddock Way
Storth
Cumbria
LA7 7JJ

Invoice		5773
Date		15/11/2012
Account No.		FSHA105
Order No.		0543

Quantity	Product Description	Net Amount	VAT Amount
1.00	Repair to main bathroom toilet	29.00	5.80

PLEASE SEND PAYMENTS TO:-

Pure Leisure
Fellend Caravan Park
Slackhead Road
Hale
Milnthorpe
LA7 7BS
Telephone: 015395 62122

Net Amount	29.00
VAT Amount	5.80
Invoice Total	34.80

PLOT NO 199
KEN SHAW AND SUE BARTON

SEPTIMUS COOPER
FROM INFORMATION
MADE AVAILABLE
TO HIM, SPRING 2014.

28.12.11	PURCHASE	- £26,834.50
FEB 14	BUY-BACK	- £ 4,500.00
28 MONTH	LOSS	- £22,334.50

2012 to 2013	ESTIMATED COST OF IMPROVEMENTS BY K & S TO CARAVAN	£ 2,000.00
15.11.12 / 7.1.13 / 6.4.13	REPAIRS & REPLACEMENTS	£ 159.60
10.11 / 02.12	SITE FEES	£ 6,965.62
12.2.2013	INSURANCE	£ 470.99
2012	ELECTRICITY	£ 488.62
2013	" EST.	£ 500.00
12.2.2013	GAS (EST)	£ 1,250.00

£ 33,529.33

THIS FINAL FIGURE EQUATES TO £276.34 PR. WEEK

BASED ON A 28 MONTH PERIOD OF RESIDENCY.

02.06.2014
(SEPTIMUS COOPER)

9. Bill and Anne

Bill and Anne Moore arrived on the park in 2005 as "full-timers". They purchased a 2001 Pemberton Montreux Caravan. It was sited on plot number sixty nine. They paid £25,000 (twenty-five thousand pounds) for this three year old unit. Due to ill health they left the park three years later and the resultant buy-back transaction yielded them £10,000 (ten thousand pounds). Yes, a virtual depreciation of £100 (one hundred pounds) per week. Bill and Anne Moore will confirm this in writing if necessary. NB: This sale and buy-back is relevant to my next revelation concerning Kevin Cattle and Sue Pearson, in sale and buy-back number ten.

10. Kevin and Sue

Kevin and Sue moved onto Fell End Park in 2008, where they had purchased for cash a new A.B.I. Roselle caravan for £38,000 (thirty eight thousand pounds). This was by way of two cheques, one for £3,000 (three thousand pounds) and one for £35,000 (thirty five thousand pounds). The deposit and the balance respectively.

In early course Sue found the slight but long incline to their new home very tiring. She was in fact not in the best of health, and being 'full-timers' didn't help matters either. They duly asked for the caravan to be transferred to a plot which did not pose this problem. They were advised that this was not possible. A Mr. Crowe classic now begins to emerge. He just happened to have the *very* caravan to suit their needs: it being the caravan bought back by Fell End off Bill and Anne Moore. This is referred to in the sale and buy-back transaction reference number nine. Being a trusting couple, but in this instance also foolishly credulous, Kevin and Sue fell for Mr. Crowe's cunning, audacious, astonishing trap. Hook, line and sinker – lambs to the slaughter they went; now the owners, due to a straight swap, of a caravan six years older than the new one they had left.

They moved into the new A.B.I. Roselle caravan on the 22nd August 2008, and "about three months later" into the six year old Pemberton Montreux. Kindly note the invoice in respect of the Pemberton has a date of 06.09.08 which is fair enough. The invoice (as with the Pemberton) has no number and is also dated 06.09.08 and showing a balance due of £35,000 (thirty-five thousand pounds). Printed names, not signed on behalf of Pure

Leisure by (birds of a feather?) Mr. Crowe and his son Mr. Ben Crowe. It also states with emphasis the following, "this is a straight exchange for the A.B.I. Roselle and we will supply FOC 2 x 19kg gas bottles for new van". How can the two invoices have the same dates? Why is there a balance due still showing in respect of the Pemberton? Copies of the two invoices are shown herein.

The sale and buy-back transactions reference numbers nine and ten deserve highlighting as follows (and although I appreciate you are already gasping at the Pure Leisure/Fell End Park profits against these two caravans, my calculations confirm the following):

Replacement Schedule
2005: Bill and Anne paid for the Pemberton: £25,000
2008: Bill and Anne received (buy-back) for same: £10,000
Fell End Park profit: £15,000
2008 Kevin and Sue paid for A.B.I/Pemberton: £38,000
2013 Kevin and Sue received (buy-back) for Pemberton: £3,000
 Fell End Park profit: £35,000
Total Profit on two caravans: £50,000

Plus profits on these two units in respect of sales/buy-backs "gone by and yet to come"! It must also be taken into account and deducted from the total profit the cost of two gas bottles provided F.O.C. in respect of Kevin's move to the Pemberton.

Confirmation (herein) from the A.B.I. Roselle Caravan manufacturers proves a recommended retail price of £20,400 (twenty-thousand four hundred pounds). In actual fact, their reference to the serial number 1330065 matches the serial number shown on the Fell End Park's non-numbered invoice of £38,000 (thirty-eight thousand pounds). Indeed, the caravan industries 'bible' Glasses price guide confirms the figure of £20,400. Proof beyond doubt as to the caravan's proper value.

Herein is a copy of the Pure Leisure Group's (no – not the Fell End Park's) 'customer leaving site' form, dated the 24th January 2013, *not* signed by either Kevin or Sue. Oddly it shows the year of the Pemberton as "2002/4". This form proves the *group* paid them the sum of £3,000 (three-thousand pounds) for their caravan. This form was produced some time after they had been "forced off" the park. This came about when Mr. Crowe called uninvited at their Morecambe accommodation with as cash 'settlement'.

Evidently Kevin and Sue had been protesting for some time as to the buy-back offer of £3,000. Rightly or wrongly they refused to pay the annual site fee deposit of £500 due in October 2012.

The aforementioned unsigned 'leaving' form is, you will notice, virtually blank. This making it, I suggest, an illegal and worthless document.

It is now a year since I have been able to contact this lovely couple (their telephone number is no longer available). At that time Sue informed me they were living in sheltered accommodation. Kevin however was being intermittently committed to a psychiatric hospital.

At our last meeting over lunch in Morecambe Sue's final words were as follows: "We're living in hope we may see the day when the Fell End Park is publically brought to justice". I hope one day my book comes into their possession – as I had promised them.

This brings an end to the 'Sales and Buy-backs' section of the book. It proves to me the presence of totally blatant unadulterated financial malpractices constantly in operation due to the Park's pure pillaging policy.

Fell End Caravan Park
Slackhead Road, Hale, Milnthorpe, LA7 7BS
Tel: 015395 62122   Fax: 015395 63810

PERSONAL DETAILS – "Holiday Home Owner" or "Customer" including permanent address

PLEASE COMPLETE IN BLACK INK & BLOCK CAPITALS

Sale No:

Name: MR KEVIN CATTLE
Address: 99 CLERENDEN ROAD MORECAMBE

Postcode: LA3 1SB   Tel No: 01524 424250

PART EXCHANGE DETAILS

Unit Checked by:		
Make:	Model:	
Size:	Beds:	Pitch No:
Serial No:	Stock No:	Year:
Finance Company	Agreement no:	
Settlement Figure: £	Valid To (date)	

Insurance: It is a requirement of your Site Licence that you maintain adequate insurance on your holiday home. This can be arranged by Pure Leisure if required. If you choose to make alternative insurance arrangements you must submit a copy of your Insurance Certificate to the Park Office on completion.

By signing this document you agree (i) to purchase the Holiday Home on the terms & conditions at the price shown (ii) that you will not have ownership, tenancy or other proprietary interest in the pitch on which the Holiday Home is sited (iii)* to part exchange your Holiday Home which you confirm is your property, free from any Hire purchase/conditional sale agreement, charge, lien or third party claim of any kind except as stated on this document
NOTES/ADDITIONAL ITEMS INCLUDED WITH THE SALE

CAN KEEP EXISTING METAL SHED , DEREK TO MODIFY WORKTOP TO ACCOMMODATE FRIDGE FREEZER

Signature (Customer(s):

Signed: ANDY CROWE   & on behalf of Pure Leisure   Date: 6/09/2008

FOR OFFICE USE ONLY				PRINT NAME:	ANDY CROWE
	Holiday Home SIV	£	Part Exchange SIV	£	
	Yes |		Approved By (Park/Sales Manager)	Finance	£

Fell End Caravan Park is operated as a Holiday Park and your attention is drawn to the fact that holiday homes cannot be occupied during the closed season each year, excepting the details outlined in your copy of the Park Rules. The holiday home may not be used except for holiday or recreational accommodation and there is no right to reside in or use the same as your only or main residence. This is a legally binding agreement which you should only sign if you are satisfied with its terms & conditions. You should understand that the purchase price of the Holiday Home and any resale value are subject to a variety of factors and resale value may reduce or increase over time.

pure leisure

HOLIDAY HOME DETAILS

Year: 2008

Make: ABI   Model: ROSELLE
Size: 36 X12   Beds: 2
Current Location: 257   Serial/Chassis No. 1330065
New Location: 257   Stock No: 246

Source of Sale: transferred sale from LLV

	Incl.	To be invoiced
Purchase Price: £38000		
Site Fees £ inc remainder 2008		
Trade In Allowance (subject to cond. year) (£)		
Deposit: Cash £	Siting & Connection	√
	Rates	
(Deposits are non-returnable) C/Card £	Steps	
Cheque £	Fridge (new/used)	Fridge freezer
Transferred from LLv Gress 27 £3000	Skirting	
	Decking	
Finance:	Gas Bottles – detail no. & size	2 x19
TOTAL TO FINANCE (if applicable) £	Gas Regulator/Hose ADDITIONAL ITEMS TO BE INVOICED LAST	inc
Total Balance Due: £3000		
(Deposits are non-refundable) Deposit Outstanding £		
Completion Date: ASAP approx 2 weeks		

ABI (UK) LIMITED
Swinemoor Lane Beverley
East Yorkshire HU17 0LJ
Tel: 01482 862976

5th June 2014

Mr S. Cooper
Estuary View
Milnthorpe
Cumbria
LA2 7DT

ABI Roselle 36.12.2B 2008 s/no 1330065

Dear Mr Cooper,

Following our telephone conversation Thursday 29th May 2014, I now have pleasure in writing to confirm as requested, the recommended manufacturers retail price for the above mentioned holiday home (at time of manufacture) which was £20,400.00 including VAT. This price would not include any optional extras.

I hope this is sufficient for your needs.

Kind regards

Diane Ashton
Warranty & Customer Services Manager
Dd – 01482 678007
Diane.ashton@abiuk.co.uk

Int: +44 1482 862976
Fax: 01482 871482
Sales/After Sales Tel: 01482 678000
Sales/After Sales Fax: 01482 887009
Email: info@abiuk.co.uk
Website: www.abiuk.co.uk

Registered Office: Swinemoor Lane
Beverley East Yorkshire HU17 0LJ
Registered in England No. 3053786

Fell End Caravan Park
Slackhead Road, Hale, Milnthorpe, LA7 7BS
Tel: 015395 62122 Fax: 015395 63810

Sale No:

PLEASE COMPLETE IN BLACK INK & BLOCK CAPITALS

PERSONAL DETAILS – "Holiday Home Owner" or "Customer" including permanent address
Name: MR KEVIN CATTLE
Address: 99 CLERENDEN ROAD MORECAMBE
Postcode: LA3 158   Tel No: 01524 424250

Unit Checked by:

HOLIDAY HOME DETAILS

Make: PEMBERTON	Model: MOTREUX	
Size: 38 X12	Beds: 2	Year: 2002
Current Location: 69		
New Location: 69	Serial/Chassis No:	
	Stock No: 490	

Source of Sale: transferred sale from LLV

			Incl.	To be invoiced
Purchase Price:	£ 38000	Siting & Connection		
Site Fees	£ inc remainder 2008	Rates	y	
Trade In Allowance: (subject to cont. year)	(£)	Steps		
Deposit:		Fridge (new/used)		
	Cash £	Skirting	Fridge freezer	
(Deposits are non-refundable)	C/Card £	Decking		
	Cheque £	Gas Bottles – detail no. & size	2 x19	
	Transferred from LLv Gross 27	Gas Reg-in-on/Hose ADDITIONAL ITEMS TO BE INVOICED - LIST	inc	
Finance:				
TOTAL TO FINANCE (if applicable)	£			
Total Balance Due:	£35000			
(Deposits are non-refundable)	Deposit Outstanding £			

Completion Date: ASAP approx 2 weeks

PART EXCHANGE DETAILS

Make: Model:
Size: Beds: Pitch No:
Serial No: Stock No: Year:
Finance Company: Agreement no:
Settlement Figure: £   Valid To (date):

Insurance: It is a requirement of your Site Licence that you maintain adequate insurance on your holiday home. This can be arranged by Pure Leisure if required. If you choose to make alternative insurance arrangements you must submit a copy of your Insurance Certificate to the Park Office on completion.

By signing this document you agree (i) to purchase the Holiday Home on the terms & conditions at the price shown (ii) that you will not have ownership, tenancy or other proprietary interest in the pitch on which the Holiday Home is sited (iii) to part exchange your Holiday Home which you confirm is your property, free from any hire purchase/conditional sale agreement, charge, lien or third party claim of any kind except as stated on this document
This is a straight exchange for the ABI rowella and we will supply FOC 2 x19kg gas bottles for new van

Fell End Caravan Park is operated as a Holiday Park and your attention is drawn to the fact that holiday homes cannot be occupied during the closed season each year, excepting the details outlined in your copy of the Park Rules. The holiday home may not be used except for holiday or recreational accommodation and there is no right to reside in or use the same as your only or main residence. This is a legally binding agreement which you should only sign if you are satisfied with its terms & conditions. You should understand that the purchase price of the Holiday Home and any resale value are subject to a variety of factors and resale value may reduce or increase over time.

Signature (Customer): [signature]
Signed: ANDY CROWE   Date: 6/09/2008
                                                 PRINT NAME: BEN CROWE

FOR OFFICE USE ONLY

✓ or X	Holiday Home SIV	£	& on behalf of Pure Leisure		
✓ or X	Part Exchange SIV	£			
	Approved By (Park/Sales Manager):		Finance	£	

CUSTOMER LEAVING SITE FORM

pure leisure

This form is to be completed by the Park Manager with the Customer.

Park: FELL END	Pitch No: 69
Name: SUE PEARSON & KEVIN CATTLE	Holiday Home Make: PEMBERTON
Address: 99 CLARENDEN ROAD MORCAMBE	Model: MONTREUX
	Size: 36X12
	No of bedrooms: 2
Postcode:	Year: 2002/4
Date:	Stock

Reason for Leaving - please tick as appropriate

☐ **Owner Unit Leaving Park**   YES

I/we hereby give 28 days notice of my/our wish to remove our caravan from the park on the agreed date of .... I/we understand all monies due to Pure Leisure / Pure Leisure Estates Ltd, including the disconnection charge, must be paid in full before the holiday home may be removed from the park.

☐ **Holiday Home Sold on Private Sale**

In accordance with the Private Sale Agreement attached and signed by me/us we hereby agree to Pure Leisure / Pure Leisure Estates Ltd to deduct all/any monies owing to them, the balance being remitted to me/us in full and final settlement for all outstanding claims that exist or might arise between us.

Price received for private sale of holiday home:	£3000 TRADE	New Customer Sales Order No:

☐ **Buy Back/Abandonment**

I/we declare the above holiday home is my/our property free from any Hire Purchase agreement, charge, lien or encumbrance of any kind except as detailed below. I/we agree to sell our holiday home to Pure Leisure / Pure Leisure Estates Ltd in its present condition as inspected by the Company representative for the sum set out below (the price includes equipment, gas cylinder and paving slabs). Pure Leisure / Pure Leisure Estates Ltd will deduct all/any monies owing to them, the balance being remitted to me/us in full and final settlement for all outstanding claims that exist or might arise between us. *(Used Unit Checklist to be completed prior to agreement – copy to be attached)*

Unit Checked By:		
Price agreed for buy-back of holiday home:		PLG HAVE WAVED THE DISCONNECTION FEE AS A FINAL GESTURE OF GOOD WILL
Monies outstanding on HP Agreement as at	*(insert date)*	

The payment of £3000 and the gesture of free disconnection and removal are made in acceptance that Mr Cattle or Mrs Pearson accept these sums of money as full and final settlement of all and any issues between themselves and Pure leisure and that any future claims will not be made against Pure Leisure, Fell End Caravan park or any of the company's employees or representatives.

Signed by customer / 24/01/2013   24/01/2013   signed for PLG

☐ **Finance Repossession**

Notification from the finance company is attached. Please note, in this instance only the Customer Leaving Site Form does not need to be signed by the Registered Owner.

EFFECTIVE DATE OF LEAVING	24/01/2013	
FINAL ELECTRIC METER READING	Electric Reading	
FINAL GAS METER READING (IF APPLICABLE) Please complete as appropriate	Cubic Meter Reading	Cubic Foot Reading

Signed: .... Registered Owner   Date: 24/01/2013

Signed: .... Park Manager   Date: 24/01/2013

Remittances will be dealt with by the Finance Department and you should allow a minimum of 21 days from the date of signing this form before receiving your remittance.

FOR PARK MANAGEMENT USE:

Used Unit Checklist Completed & Attached:	Price Agreed as Above & Authorised by Area Manager (signature/date)	

FOR FINANCE DEPARTMENT USE:

Last Updated 19.01.07

16. NO SALE, NO BUY-BACK

Paul decided to remove his caravan from Fell End Park in late 2014. It is relevant to know the park's new 2014/2015 regulations. Before I recount the resultant, bitter experience he had to endure, these are as follows:

Rule 4 Clause 4.13

"Any owner who wishes to remove a holiday home from the park must give Pure Leisure 14 days notice of removal. Pure Leisure must carry out disconnection of the services and make ready to remove. A reasonable charge will be made for this service. All monies due to Pure Leisure must be paid before the holiday home is removed from the park."

Rule 18 Clause 18.2

Part of which states: "Pure Leisure is entitled to write to you and require you to remove the holiday home from the park within one month"

Rule 18 Clause 18.3

Part of which states: "You must remove the holiday home and all other property of yours from the park".

Rule 18 Clause 18.5

"If following the termination of the license agreement you fail to arrange the removal of the holiday home, Pure Leisure is entitled to do so and recover the cost of the removal from the disposal of the holiday home as it sees fit".

It will be observed that no mention at all is made in the rulings of a charge by Pure Leisure i.e. whenever the caravan is removed by the resident of a certain holiday park. Fell End Park. Paul was informed that his caravan had no buy-back value whatsoever. He therefore decided to remove his caravan himself upon advising the park's management (guess who?). He was informed that any removal had to be carried out by the park themselves: at a charge of £950.00 (nine hundred and fifty pounds).

See rule 18, clause 18.5 – once again its 'fill your boots' time for the park, although from my observations even this expression comes nowhere near describing the plunderous depths Fell End more often reached than not. This ruling makes no mention should a disposal/sales figure exceed the removal charge. One would have thought that in all probability Fell End would try to retain the unit on site. They wouldn't enjoy their "removal fee" from a trade buyer and furthermore a healthy retail price coupled with annual site fees would then be obtained. Or, alternatively, the option to rent out.

On the 12th December 2014, not long after Paul's withdrawal from the park, I held a conversation with Karen, and official of the firm Titans Siting and Transport, based in Northamptonshire. Work takes this company all over the United Kingdom, plus France and Spain. A leader in its field. I requested a hypothetical estimate with regards to Paul's removal i.e. if Titan were based say 'next door' to Fell End. A figure of £250 to £300 plus V.A.T. was quoted. This figure would take into account a distance of up to one mile, the subject of removal being a thirty-eight foot by twelve foot caravan.

Some years earlier Fell End agreed to remove Paul's caravan to another plot, away from the nightly blaring of the music coming from the adjacent leisure complex. This removal and re-siting was 'clocked' by Paul, it taking 45 minutes with two men involved. He calculated that on the basis of £950 per removal the charge per man per hour (and I agree with him) would be £633.

Paul had paid all his dues to the park over a period of time of ten years. He was a regular patron of the park's leisure facilities. An asset, in a way, to Fell End. He had now been made to become a disconsolate, disillusioned, angry young man. Having been in his company on many an occasion over several years I know his strength of character will ensure that these feelings will soon fade. Though not the memory.

Like many others he had become ensnared, left only possessing an emotion of hopelessness.

It is now February 2015. One of my moles informs me the caravan in question is still on site. Awaiting the buying season?

17. THE ELECTRICITY FRAUD – PART ONE

Energy Cost Management Ltd. (E.C.M.), as you will see from their letter to me dated the 16th April 2009 and the Pure Leisure Group's (P.L.G.) letter to a park resident, Mr. Harry McKearney, dated the 27th October 2008 *provide and purchase electricity for PLG's "whole group of sites"*. Thus, of course, ensuring each and every park are charged the same tariff. E.C.M.'s letter and other correspondence also highlights the following:

Rate Charged	2008	2009	2010	2011
E.C.M.	7.06	12.63	12.63	*not known
P.L.G.	12.63	13.39	15.26	14.53

With regard to E.C.M.'s letter dated the 20th April 2010, this complete turnaround in contrast to their previous cooperation was obviously due to a "batten down the hatches" order from P.L.G.

*During April/May 2012 E.C.M. were asked in writing on three occasions to confirm the unit price they charged P.L.G. for the year 2011. They eventually replied as follows: "E.C.M. Ltd is engaged by Pure Leisure Group to advise the group on energy and water management issues. I have asked their accounts department what they charge at Fell End and have been told it is 14.53p/kWh". Blatantly obvious this is not the answer I requested. Further prodding correspondence from me resulted in them 'running to' P.L.G. whereupon their managing director a Mr. A. Fox duly telephoned me and proposed we came to a settlement (more of this is explained later in the book, as is the deepening of the 'in cahoots' situation between E.C.M. and P.L.G.). At the end of this little bout of exchanges the question remains – if E.C.M had charged P.L.G. 14.53p/kWh, the former's reply would have been all so simple.

ENERGY COST MANAGEMENT
Delivering solutions to minimise costs

·ECM·

Mr A S Cooper
255 Fell End Caravan Park
Slackhead Lane
Hale
Milnthorpe
Cumbria
LA7 7BS

16th April 2009

Dear Mr. Cooper

RE- Increase in Electricity Prices

Thank you for your letter regarding the increase in Electricity Prices in 2008.

As you will be aware from all the press coverage last year, Britain saw some of the highest energy prices that we have ever had, with all suppliers increasing the rates in both the domestic & commercial markets.

We are the Energy Consultants for the Pure Leisure Group and last year we tendered the group of sites to all Major Suppliers to gain the most competitive market prices. With the Energy market being as it was, getting the best price was a major priority.

Suppliers purchase their Energy on the wholesale energy market and everyday these prices vary. At one point the base price was trading at over 9p / KWH. This was at the Power Station gate, without any distribution or transmission costs, or any supplier cost for metering, billing and profit, which must all be added to form the retail price at your meter.

Pure Leisure had signed a two year Electricity contract in 2006 at low rates and this contract was due for renewal last year when prices where at the highest, therefore;-

The Contract signed in 2006 gave you your price at 7.06p
The Contract signed in 2008 gives you your current price at 12.63p

Energy Cost Management Ltd, The Old Printworks, Birley Street, Kirkham, Preston PR4 2AT
telephone: 01772 682323   facsimile: 01772 686080   solutions@ecm-uk.com   www.ecm-uk.com
registered in england and wales, company reg no. 337082   vat no: 693287393

YOUR PARTNER IN UTILITY COST REDUCTION

· E C M ·

The Wholesale market increase has been up to 100%, and as you have stated in your letter your increase, although substantial, is less than that amount. This is due to the purchasing power of Pure Leisure's whole group of sites, ECM's tendering process, and it compares favourably with other offers.

I hope this helps to clarify why you have seen such an increase in your costs and I can assure you that Pure Leisure and ECM go to great lengths to ensure you get the best deal possible at every Contract renewal.

yours sincerely

M. Gaskell

Marion Gaskell
Senior Account Manager

pure leisure
GROUP
UK & INTERNATIONAL HOLIDAY HOMES

Mr McKearney
17 College Road North
Blundellsands
Merseyside
L23 8UP

27th October 2008

Dear Mr McKearney

Thank you for your recent query with regard to your electricity bill.

We use a company of energy consultants in Kirkham to purchase our electricity contracts. The reason for this is that they buy in bulk for the company all our electrical energy needs and contract forward for a suitable time. The present contract, like the last will be in effect for two years. As with the previous contract, I am sure that you will be happy with the price in a further year..

If you wish to speak to our energy advisers, their address is:

Energy Cost Management Ltd.
The Old Printworks, Birley Street,
Kirkham, Preston. Lancashire
PR4 2AT

You can contact them on 01772 682323 and they will be delighted to speak to you.

Yours sincerely

Alan Green

PURE LEISURE GROUP
South Lakeland House
Yealand Redmayne, Carnforth
Lancashire. LA5 9RN. UK.

t: +44 (0) 1524 781918
f: +44 (0) 1524 782243
e: enquiries@pureleisuregroup.com
t: www.pureleisuregroup.com
Company No. 05113715

ENERGY COST MANAGEMENT
Delivering solutions to minimise costs

·E C M·

Mr A S Cooper
255 Fell End Caravan Park
Slackhead Lane
Hale
Milnthorpe
Cumbria
LA7 7BS

11th May 2009

Dear Mr. Cooper

RE- Increase in Electricity Prices

I must apologise for not responding to you to your letter dated 20th April.

The contract for 2008 as a start date of August and unfortunately we didn't negotiate the earlier contract for this site, I would advise you to contact Alan Green for this information.

Again please accept my apology for not replying by return

yours sincerely

Marion Gaskell
Senior Account Manager

Energy Cost Management Ltd, The Old Printworks, Birley Street, Kirkham, Preston PR4 2AT
telephone: 01772 682323   facsimile: 01772 686080   solutions@ecm-uk.com   www.ecm-uk.com
registered in england and wales, company reg no. 3377082   vat no: 693287393

YOUR PARTNER IN UTILITY COST REDUCTION

ENERGY COST MANAGEMENT
Delivering solutions to minimise costs

·ECM·

Mr A S Cooper
255 Fell End Caravan Park
Slackhead Lane
Hale
Milnthorpe
Cumbria
LA7 7BS

6th July 2009

Dear Mr. Cooper

RE- Increase in Electricity Prices

Thank you for your letter regarding the increase in Electricity Prices in 2008.

I am sorry but I do not get involved with the re-charging that Pure Leisure does for their customers.

You may wish to contact them direct.

yours sincerely

M. Gaskell

Marion Gaskell
Senior Account Manager

Energy Cost Management Ltd, The Old Printworks, Birley Street, Kirkham, Preston PR4 2AT
telephone: 01772 682323   facsimile: 01772 686080   solutions@ecm-uk.com   www.ecm-uk.com
registered in england and wales, company reg no. 3577082   vat no: 693287393

YOUR PARTNER IN UTILITY COST REDUCTION

ENERGY COST MANAGEMENT · E C M ·

Delivering solutions to minimise costs

Mr A S Cooper
255 Fell End Caravan Park
Slackhead Lane
Hale
Milnthorpe
Cumbria
LA7 7BS

20th April 2010

Dear Mr. Cooper

Request for Copy Correspondence

Thank you for your letter dated 1st April, asking for copies of correspondence during 2009.

Energy Cost Management Ltd. Is engaged by Pure Leisure Group to advise the Group on Energy and Water related issues. I am therefore unable to enter discussions with you or exchange correspondence without their consent.

I have made the Group aware of your request and I have been informed that the file is now closed on this matter.

yours sincerely

Marion Gaskell
Senior Account Manager

Energy Cost Management Ltd, The Old Printworks, Birley Street, Kirkham, Preston PR4 2AT
telephone: 01772 682323   facsimile: 01772 686080   solutions@ecm-uk.com   www.ecm-uk.com
registered in england and wales, company reg no. 3377082 vat no: 693287393

YOUR PARTNER IN UTILITY COST REDUCTION

THE ELECTRICITY FRAUD PART ONE - CONTINUED

The leading Pure Leisure Group LTD. culprits directly and indirectly involved in the electric fraud in alphabetical order and together with their titles/functions are as follows:

Period of Office

18.12.09 – 25.04.14: Mr Anthony Fox – Managing Director – Board member

2004 – 2012: Mr. Alan Green – Communications – Director

07.07.04 – Current: Mr. John Morphet – Chairman – Owner

09.07.06 – 03.02.14: Mr. Christopher Royle – Group Solicitor and Company Secretary

2006 – Current: Mr. Trevor White – Corporate Affairs – Director

You will become aware of their detailed involvement as the book progresses with the fraud study theme.

I attempted to start the ball rolling with my letter (shown herein – appendix A) dated the 20th October 2008. This was followed by seven further letters (all with recorded delivery status) between then and 9th December 2009. In addition to these was one sent direct to chairman/owner of the Fell End Park, Mr. J. Morphet, which was dated 20th January 2010. A reply to this letter was in fact received from Mr. T. White, director of corporate affairs, dated the 1st February 2010 (appendix B. herein). I replied, having been indisposed, on the 12th March 2010 (appendix C) and the 17th March (appendix D). Mr White responded to these on the 25th March 2010 (appendix E). Finally I replied in harsh tones to him on the 6th April 2010 (appendix F) to which no answer was received. To me, this person's cowardly, weak defence was quite foreseeable partly due to his virtually impossible task of representing lies versus the truth. Exactly two weeks to the day after Mr. White's letter to me, i.e. on the 8th April 2010, the local press ran an article under the heading 'EXEC FILE'. Its subject being Trevor White which, when he was asked his personal skills, the following answer was printed: "communication skills, both written and verbal, are an absolute essential in the Leisure industry – after all, we are selling a lifestyle". Also, part of his answer to the question "what qualifications do you possess", came the reply – "the school of life".

Kindly now refer to my letters of the 27th April and the 12th May 2010, appendices G and H respectively. The combined effect of this correspondence finally elicited a response dated 25th May 2010. No, not from Mr. Green but a certain Mr. Royle ("Chris Royle"), appendix J, who held the grandiose title of Group Solicitor and Company Secretary. He obviously having 'replaced' the guilt-ridden?, hapless, ignoramus Mr. Green, brother-in-law of the Park's owner. Whatever; I felt progress was now to be made – oh, my gross naivety!

APPENDIX (A)

20th October 2008

<u>Typed Copy of Original Handwritten Letter</u>

<u>Unit 255</u>
<u>Fell End Caravan Park</u>

<u>Re: Invoice 1340</u>
<u>Electric Account</u>

Dear Sirs,

I note an increase of 76.5% regarding this years unit price compared with your invoice 318 of 20/08/07.

Is this correct and if so could you kindly explain.

Thanking You.

Yours Faithfully,

Mr Septimus Cooper

Pure Leisure Group
South Lakeland House
A6
Yealand Redmayne
Carnforth
Lancashire
LA5 9RN

APPENDIX (B)

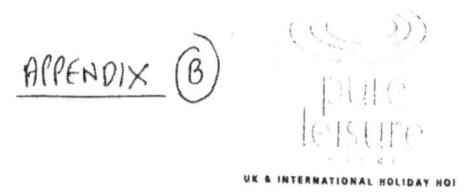

Mr Septimus Cooper
Links View
Mayfield Avenue
Ingol
Preston
Lancs
PR2 3PL

1st February 2010

Dear Mr Cooper,

I am in receipt of you letter dated 20th January 2010 addressed for the personal attention of Mr John Morphet, Pure Leisure Group Chairman, to which Mr Morphet has asked me to respond.

I have read the additional correspondence attached to this letter and discussed the points raised with Alan Green, Operations Director. My understanding is that he has written to you (letter dated 16th October 2009) and requested clarification of the electricity invoice that you wish to query and that you have responded stating that your earlier letters outline that query.

The correspondence that I have consists of photocopies of earlier letters, most of which are faint copies and difficult to read. Could I suggest that if this as this matter does not seem to have been resolved from your point of view that you respond to Mr Green's letter outlining the precise nature of your concern. I am sure if you do that then we can bring this matter to conclusion.

With regard to your comment about the letter of 20th January being the eighth you have written without response I cannot agree. Mr Green has responded to the addresses which we had on file, both at Fell end Caravan Park and Staveley.

PURE LEISURE GROUP

+44 (0) 1524 781918
+44 (0) 1524 782243

APPENDIX (B) (CONT.)

The address that you have currently supplied on your most recent letters displays an incorrect postcode which reads – PR2 23PL – this is for Perivale, London, whereas the correct postcode for Ingol, Preston should read - PR2 3PL. This also may explain why letters have gone astray.

Yours sincerely,

Trevor White
Director of Corporate Affairs.

APPENDIX (C)

Mr Trevor White
Director of Corporate Affairs
Pure Leisure Group
South Lakeland House
Yealand Redmayne
Carnforth
Lancashire
LA5 9RN

12th March 2010

Dear Mr White,

Thank you for your letter of the 1st February 2010, I regret the delay in replying due to circumstances beyond my control.

I agree to receipt of Mr Greens correctly post-coded letter (dated 6th October 2009) sent to my Staveley address in error. This was received together with a copy attached to a compliment slip (and apology) dated 27th October 2009 on the 28th October 2009. I replied to this in my letter (11th November 2009) in which I referred to my concerns detailed in my letter of 7th July 2009. This, plus the copy correspondence between myself and your Electricity Suppliers E.C.M. (in your possession), surely explains fully the reasons for my concerns regarding the overcharging of electricity supplied.

As suggested by yourselves I am quite prepared to respond to Mr Greens letter but this is only duplicating matters, I would respectfully ask you to read the E.C.M. correspondence and my letter (7th July 2009) together with Mr Green, whereby I am sure you will then fully understand my concerns. I trust you will agree on this point, if not I will gladly forward to Mr Green copies of all correspondence to date – which to my mind already spells out the situation.

You state you have read all my correspondence and then also mention it is difficult to read, I am not sure what point you are making here. In the same context I could make the (irrelevant) point of not comprehending the first part of the second sentence of your third paragraph, and indeed your mis-spelling of 'Fell End'.

To complete my file, would you kindly let me have copies of all your replies to my letters and would you also provide evidence that PR2 23PL is the post code for Perivale, London, as you intimate, this may explain why letters have gone astray.

Kindly find enclosed photo copies of seven stamped and franked envelopes posted by the writer to his Preston address with the incorrect post code from various parts of Cumbria, Lancashire and Cheshire on consecutive days and over an eight day period, all of which were delivered without any hitch.

I thank you in anticipation of your reply.

Yours Sincerely,

Septimus Cooper

(1ST COPY)

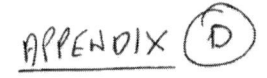

APPENDIX D

1st Class Recorded Delivery

Links View
Mayfield Avenue
Ingol
Preston
Lancashire
PR2 3PL

Wednesday 17th March 2010

Dear Mr White,

Further to my letter of the 12th March 2010, I incorrectly referred to Mr Green's letter of the 16th October 2009 as the 6th October 2009, for which I apologise.

Whilst writing would you explain how and why Mr Green's forementioned letter, which you have since sent to me, was presumably returned to you by the post office.

I ask this in view of a six-month re-direction order to my Preston address for all Staveley addressed mail being in force from the 28th August 2009 to the 7th March 2010. Written proof can be provided.

I await your advice on this very important point.

Yours Sincerely,

Septimus Cooper

Mr Trevor White
Director of Corporate Affairs
Pure Leisure Group
South Lakeland House
Yealand Redmayne
Carnforth
Lancashire
LA5 9RN

APPENDIX E

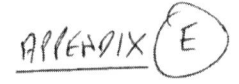

pure leisure
UK & INTERNATIONAL HOLIDAY HOMES

Mr Septimus Cooper
Links View
Mayfield Avenue
Ingol
Preston
Lancs
PR2 3PL

25th March 2010

Dear Mr Cooper,

I am in receipt of your letters dated 12th & 17th March 2010 and would draw your attention to paragraph 3 of my letter to you dated 1st February................................

The correspondence that I have consists of photocopies of earlier letters, most of which are faint copies and difficult to read. Could I suggest that as this matter does not seem to have been resolved from your point of view that you respond to Mr Green's letter outlining the precise nature of your concern. I am sure if you do that then we can bring this matter to conclusion.

I see little value in going over old ground regarding dates when earlier correspondence was received or not and at which address, nor do I see any gain in commenting on specific points in isolation within that correspondence. The simplest route to resolving this issue is outlined above so please respond as requested.

Yours sincerely,

Trevor White
Director of Corporate Affairs

PURE LEISURE GROUP

South Lakeland House
Yealand Redmayne, Carnforth
Lancashire. LA5 9RN. UK.

t: +44 (0) 1524 781918
f: +44 (0) 1524 782243
e: enquiries@pureleisuregroup.com
i: www.pureleisuregroup.com

Company No. 05113719

APPENDIX (F)   9/4/10

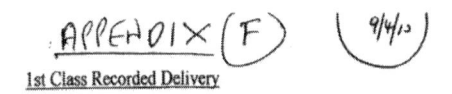

1st Class Recorded Delivery

Links View
Mayfield Avenue
Ingol
Preston
PR2 3PL

6th April 2010

Dear Mr White,

With reference to your letter of the 25th March 2010, it appears obvious that you are not prepared to face up and answer the points raised in my letters of the 12th and 17th March 2010, and indeed I find your ultimate paragraph totally unacceptable.
Should all the correspondence ever be laid bare on neutral ground then I believe that contents of the same revealed therein would prove to be damning.
I find it puzzling as to why you should have gone to the lengths regarding the repetition, of the whole paragraph (3) you have referred to.
A letter ("without prejudice") will be sent to Mr Green in due course.

Yours Sincerely,

Septimus Cooper

Mr Trevor White
Director of Corporate Affairs
Pure Leisure Group
South Lakeland House
Yealand Redmayne
Carnforth
Lancs
LA5 9RN

27th April 2010   APPENDIX G

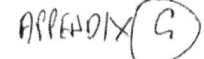

Links View
Mayfield Avenue
Ingol
Preston
PR2 3PL

Re- Electricity Charges

Dear Mr Green,

In this letter of 25th March 2010 as requested by your Mr Trevor White, I am writing to you detailing the precise nature of my concerns regarding the overcharging by Pure Leisure Group over the supply of electricity.

The complete file on this matter (from October 2008 to the present time) is enclosed including copies of the Electricity suppliers (E.C.M.)s three letters which explain the correct unit prices for the years in question and which I believe explain fully (together with previous and enclosed correspondence) the exact situation.

However I will spell out this as follows:
You will see that from the Electric Suppliers letters of the 16th April 2009 and the 11th May 2009 that the two year contract signed in August 2006 gave a unit price of 7.06p i.e. this is what should have been charged for the years ending August 2007 and August 2008. However you charged a unit price of 12.63p, Invoice no: 340 (copy enclosed) for the contract ending August 2008. For some reason, unlike previous years, your invoice was not dated (and received) in August but October (10th).

E.C.M. also state in their letter that the two year contract signed in August 2008 gave a unit price of 12.63p, i.e. this is what should be charged for the contract years ending August 2009 and August 2010. However for the contract year ending August 2009 you charged a unit price of 13.39p. Invoice No: 2242 (copy enclosed).

I would also bring to your attention the E.C.M. letter of the 6th July 2009 (copy enclosed) where they have suggested I contact you direct as "they do not get involved with the re-charging that Pure Leisure does for their customers"
Thank you in anticipation of your reply in due course.

Yours Sincerely,

Septimus Cooper

Mr Alan Green
Director of Communications
Pure Leisure Group
South Lakeland House
A6, Yealand Redmayne
Carnforth
Lancs
LA5 9RN

APPENDIX (H)
1st Class Recorded Delivery

C.C. Mr Trevor White, P.L.G.
Director of Communications

Links View
Mayfield Avenue
Ingol
Preston
Lancashire
PR2 3PL

Re-Electricity Charges

Wednesday 12th May 2010

Dear Mr Green,

I would refer to my letter of the 27th April 2010, (which was sent First Class Recorded Delivery) together with the 19 (nineteen) enclosures.

To date I have not received a reply.

I trust you will understand therefore, particularly since I have been attempting to resolve this matter for nearly one and a half years, that I am, in the protection of my interests, instructing solicitors to commence legal proceedings against the Pure Leisure Group. This action will take place on or about the 1st June 2010.

Yours Sincerely,

Septimus Cooper

Mr Alan Green
Director of Communications
Pure Leisure Group
South Lakeland House
A6, Yealand Redmayne
Carnforth
Lancashire
LA5 9RN

Mr S Cooper

Links View

Mayfield Avenue

Ingol

Preston

PR1 3PL

25ᵀᴴ May 2010

Dear Mr Cooper

Complaint re electricity charges

Alan Green has passed on to me his file of correspondence with you relating to the above with a request that I review the same on behalf of the Company.

This I will do as quickly as possible but please note that I am on holiday from tomorrow until 7th June next but I will deal with the same as soon as I return.

Yours sincerely

Chris Royle

Group Solicitor and Company Secretary

PURE LEISURE GROUP

+44 (0) 1524 781918
+44 (0) 1524 782243
enquiries@pureleisuregroup.com
www.pureleisuregroup.com

APPENDIX
K

pure leisure
UK & INTERNATIONAL HOLIDAY HOMES

Messrs Ratcliffe & Bibby

Castle Chambers

60 Market Street

Lancaster LA1 1HP

12TH July 2010

Ref JT/JT/COO1871/1

Dear Sirs

Your client Mr S Cooper complaint re electricity charges

I thank you for you letter of 6th July.

I have reviewed the file and was about to write to your client when I received your letter.

I am not entirely clear as to what it is that your client is claiming. Clearly he alleges that he has been overcharged for electricity (which incidentally is denied) but please will you set out the amount of the alleged overpayment and how this is calculated and I will look at his claim in detail.

Yours faithfully

Chris Royle

Group Solicitor and Company Secretary

PURE LEISURE GROUP

South Lakeland House
Yealand Redmayne, Carnforth
Lancashire, LA5 9RN, UK.

t: +44 (0) 1524 781918
f: +44 (0) 1524 782243
e: enquiries@pureleisuregroup.com
i: www.pureleisuregroup.com

You will already have observed and taken on board the well rehearsed policy (modus operandi) adopted by the Pure Leisure Management. This includes rebuffing, stonewalling, ignoring and even dishonesty. I use this latter word in the interests of diplomacy. It would appear that over a long period of time they have had success with these tactics. To me, their aim to anyone who threatens to oppose their malpractices is to "wear them down. In time they'll give up and go away". In confirmation of the foregoing this part of the story concerning the dialogue between the writer, his solicitors and Mr. Royle continued from May 2010 to November 2011. Yes, another one and a half years. I will now attempt to heavily abbreviate this correspondence which included 65 (sixty five) communications i.e.

My solicitor – 24 (twenty-four)
The writer – 23 (twenty-three)
Miscellaneous – 11 (eleven)
Pure Leisure – 7 (seven)

Contents illustrated herein are directly transcribed, word for word, from the original correspondence. I would have dearly wished to have included in this section the whole shooting match, wherein I'm confident you would come to understand my ever-increasing frustration, annoyance and at times, despair. However practical reasons prevent me from doing so. Consequently what you will now only see is a massively abbreviated account of the events which took place. Even so, I hope there is enough material provided for you to get the picture.

Mr. Royle's opening letter briefly stated he "would be reviewing my complaint regarding the electric charges on behalf of the company but note I'm on holiday until the 7th June but will deal with same as soon as I return". He didn't. I contacted solicitors who wrote to him on the 6th July 2010. Mr. Royle replied to them on 12th July, appendix K, as follows "I have reviewed the file and was about to contact your client when I received your letter", plus further drivel regarding his ignorance of my claim. He was then sent the full details on the 26th July. An e-mail was received from Mr. Royle on 16th August which read "I am awaiting Energy Cost Management's report. I am about to go on holiday until the 6th September. Hopefully the matter can be left in abeyance until then". A further email was received from Mr. Royle on the 17th

September which read as follows "E.C.M. required information which we have now supplied. We expect to respond to your client's allegations by the end of this month". On 4th October Mr. Royle wrote again, enclosing a spreadsheet created by E.C.M. which involved dates, words and figures totalling in excess of 900 (nine hundred). It must be remembered Pure Leisure are revered customers of E.C.M.. This back-scratching, extremely dubious tactic failed miserably. To me, a layman, it was self-evident the extensive data cunningly provided was indeed, and to be blunt, 'plucked out of thin air'. In fact, as you will see later E.C.M.'s efforts to prove P.L.G.'s innocence with regard to overcharging backfired on them both. Nevertheless from these so-called statistics Mr. Royle stated that "at one point unit owners were undercharged 00.05p per unit but provided no further action will be taken by him we will not seek to recover the same from your client accordingly" – yes, pathetic beyond belief.

After I had several in-depth conversations over a period of time with my solicitor he then wrote to Mr. Royle on the 8th December 2010. Mr. Royle e-mailed in reply on the 20th January 2011 wherein he stated that: "I apologise for the delay in replying but I have been away from the office and also Christmas has intervened". My solicitor wrote again to Mr. Royle on the 9th February 2011. A reply from him dated 14th February 2011 stated "the delay is much regretted and I do apologise for this. It was only recently I took over this case and consequently got to grips with the same" (I have no need to remind you of his letter to me of the 25th May *2010* mentioned previously). The contents of the rest of his prolonged letter were helpful in eventually bringing the downfall of both him and his company in respect of the fraudulent electricity overcharging. Detailed revelations of this will be disclosed later and at the appropriate time in the book, for reasons which I trust you will understand.

Mr Royle's final letter to my solicitor was received on the 10th March 2011. For some peculiar (or sinister?) reason it was dated the 7th February 2010. Why should this be so? I asked myself, too odd to be just a clerical error. Simply a glaring mistake left to be. Am I becoming paranoid whenever the name of Royle crosses my life's course? If there is evidence of paranoia in my writings I'm confident you will come to fully understand this as the story rolls on. After all the Oxford Dictionary's meaning of the word is: "abnormal tendency to suspect and mistrust others" – fair enough?

Calling upon solicitors to support my cause did the important trick of finally getting some reaction from the Pure Leisure Management. Notwithstanding this I made the decision of releasing them from their obligations as and from the 19th April 2011. No – it was nothing to do with costs. They were in fact extremely reasonable, probably realising a state pensioner with a caravan for a home probably deserved maximum economical treatment. Their involvement spanned nine months which included numerous telephone calls and many letters. Not forgetting they also had to handle a grand total of two emails and three letters during this period from Mr. Royle. I began to detect the craftiness and wiles of Fell End Park's legal representative had begun to take their toll on my youthful solicitor. Examples I could give but they serve no purpose. My notice to them requesting the cessation of their assistance was accepted with grace.

To describe to you my renewed personal efforts to bring this saga to an end I feel the enclosed copy correspondence is the obvious and best way to do so. They are highlighted with the reference letters L to R. Included in same is Mr. Royle's ambiguously dated letter (L).

Subsequent to my letter of the 1st December 2011 (appendix R) to Pure Leisure Group's Solicitor and Company Secretary I knew I might as well have sent it to the man on the moon. The Sunday Times showed an interest but nothing came of it. This was due to me not following up on the matter. The reason being that the intervention of fate arrived on the scene. Having become a little cynical and disillusioned with the way of the world I definitely needed a fillip. And this is what I got, in a huge measure. I now had a springboard from which to recommence my campaign with renewed vigour.

I can almost guarantee you will read the section of the book entitled "The Electric Fraud – Part Two" with incredulity coupled with a sense of total and utter disgust in the part played by the Pure Leisure Group. This I am holding back because I believe now is the appropriate time to give you "The Eviction" story and all that surrounded same. Sit tight!

Mr J Tomlinson
Ratcliffe & Bibby
Solicitors
Castle Chambers
60 Market Street
Lancaster LA1 1HP

7TH February 2010

WITHOUT PREJUDICE

Dear Mr Tomlinson

Your client Septimus Cooper

Thank you for your letter of 24th February.

By way of a separate transaction your client advised us that he wished to vacate his pitch at Fell End Caravan Park and accordingly requested us to buy in his caravan. A deal was agreed at a price of £13,000. Your client has vacated the caravan and passed over possession to us. We were about to account to your client for the sale proceeds of the caravan when we received a letter from him dated 3rd March in which he says he has decided not to proceed with the proposed agreement. This letter is puzzling because it goes on to give bank details in which to pay the sale proceeds which would be superfluous if the sale was not going ahead. We presume therefore that when your client says that he has decided not to proceed with the proposed agreement he means that he does not want to accept our offer to settle the electricity claim in the matter. We will therefore be paying to your clients bank account the sum of £11,287.47 in payment of the net purchase price after deduction of the outstanding electricity charges £1,712.53 to date in the next few days.

So far as the electricity claim is concerned we offered to waive the outstanding electricity charges for 2010 which amounted to £1,079.97 provided that your client would agree to cease with his claim against us for alleged overcharging of electricity for the years 2007 – 2009. In our view this was particularly generous to your client given that the amount now offered is considerably in excess of the amount claimed by your client – see your letter of 26th July last. Please note that the offer is made with a view to disposing of the claim and is without admission of liability. If the same is accepted we will forward to either you or your client a further cheque for £1,079.97. There is no need in our view to apply for a Consent Order since no proceedings have been issued. The correspondence passing between us will be evidence of the agreement in the matter

We wish to put on record that the offer to settle the electricity claim is still on the table and therefore the same should be considered by your client as a Part 36 offer a decision in respect of which should be made by your client within the next 14 days.

I await to hear from you

Yours sincerely

Chris Royle
Group Solicitor and Company Secretary

PURE LEISURE GROUP
South Lakeland House
Yealand Redmayne, Carnforth
Lancashire, LA5 9RN, UK

t: +44 (0) 1524 781918
f: +44 (0) 1524 782243
e: enquiries@pureleisuregroup.c
l: www.pureleisuregroup.com

APPENDIX
M

Mr. Septimus Cooper
1, St Anthony's Close,
Milnthorpe,
Cumbria.
LA7 7DT

May 20, 2011

RE: Eviction – No 295 Fell End Caravan Park.   7th TIMES

Dear Sir,

With reference to your letter (incorrectly?) dated 7th Feb 2010?? To Mr. Tomlinson, and received by him on the 10th March 2011. Firstly I would like to state that I am completely staggered by your opening (untruthful) sentence. I herewith outline the Facts, as to what actually took place.

Towards the end of February my son returned to the above unit, to find an eviction notice, stuck to the door, (For all to see). There was also another notice in an envelope in our mail slot at the reception. (Copies enclosed).

I forthwith contacted Mr Crowe, as requested on the notice, whom stated the following:-

1. He did not know why we had been evicted, but thought it may be in conjunction with an electricity charge dispute, (which as you know is still trying to be resolved).
2. Mr Crowe also stated that there would be a charge of £50.00 per day, whilst the caravan was held by the Pure Leisure Group (PLG).
3. Mr. Crowe went on to inform me that there would also be a disconnection/make ready to move fee. This as you will know that this fee is in the £700 - £800 region.

Should I have decided to sell privately, the proceeds of the sale, would have been subject to a %15 + VAT, commission charge by PLG, and indeed from several other residents, known to myself. The price is wrongly controlled, by PLG. (Usually at a figure well below its market value!!)

In addition the caravan's decommissioned state, with reference to the severed electricity and gas cables, etc. Plus the fact, that it would probably take a considerable amount of time to sell the caravan privately. Therefore all the forgoing's, left me with no other option, but to accede, to Mr Crowe approach, to offer to "Buy" the caravan.

Page 2

Furthermore, referring to my correspondence dated 3rd March 2011 (as mentioned in your letter) this was deliberately created to "SPELL OUT", the fact that I did not accept the proposed agreement in its entirety! It was to make, completely clear to all concerned, in writing, that I had no intention of waving the outstanding electrical charges to the sum of £1095.97, which was, in effect, A bribe by you, to try and persuade me "to cease with his claim against us" (your written words – not mine!).

The forgoing's, makes it extremely difficult for myself to understand, your comment within the final sentence of your penultimate paragraph. In fact I believe it makes a mockery of same.

You may be unaware of the grief and distress, within my family that the eviction notice and the unscrupulous process has caused, resulting, in my wife becoming very ill and depressed, not to mention the "quiet Back-lash", not only from the park residents, but also the local Milnthorpe and district folk. Were we had built up solid social connections, particular within their sporting areas.

However, I purchased the caravan from PLG, some six years ago, net of site fees at a cost of £39,000. Your offer/sale to me of £13,000 resulted in a weekly depreciation of £80. I note however that you are selling same at a price of £30,000. It is irrelevant, but interesting enough to put on record that, with the current fees, a weekly cost of £140.00 is envisaged, and net of all other overheads.

Furthermore, Mr Crowe, commented on the pristine condition of the caravan, thus deems our six years on the site that we set exemplary standards; for example, changing waist land into a "beautiful garden" (PLG's quoted words – not my own!). These standards would be confirmed by all residents and staff alike, whom knew me and my family.

I would also like to refer you to PLG's annual site license conditions and general site rules, in particular, rule 18:2, PLG has obviously and blatantly ignored, this ruling/condition.

I fully intend to take this whole wretched stressful experience, of the wrongful eviction process, to the attention of others, you will be of course notified with the detail, prior to this pending action.

I am baffled to the fact that I have had no explanation, from anyone, as to why we were evicted.

Sincerely,

Septimus Cooper.   Enclosure x 3

pure leisure
UK & INTERNATIONAL HOLIDAY HOM

Mr S Cooper

1 St Anthony's Close

Milnthorpe

Cumbria

LA7 7DT

6th June 2011

Dear Mr Cooper

re 255 Fell End Caravan Park

I acknowledge receipt of your letter dated 20th May the contents of which are noted.

I will take an early opportunity of discussing your letter with Mr Crowe when he is next in the office following which I will write to you again

Yours sincerely

Chris Royle

Group Solicitor anbd Company Secretary

PURE LEISURE GROUP

South Lakeland House
Yealand Redmayne, Carnforth
Lancashire. LA5 9RN. UK.

t: +44 (0) 1524 781918
f: +44 (0) 1524 782243
e: enquiries@pureleisuregroup.cor
i: www.pureleisuregroup.com

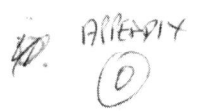

13/10/11

Mr C. Royle
Group Solicitor and Company Secretary
Pure Leisure Group
South Lakeland House
Yealand Redmayne
Carnforth
Lancashire
LA5 9RN

1 St Anthony's Close
Milnthorpe
Cumbria
LA7 7DT
015395 64053

Dear Mr Royle,

Re - Electricity Prices 255 Fell End Caravan Park

With reference to previous correspondance and in particular your letters to Messrs Ratcliffe & Bibby Solicitors, of the 4th October 2010, 14th February 2011 and 7th February 2010, the latter in reply to R&B's letter of the 24th February 2011, I would like to make the following comments.

I find it very odd, to say the least, that a review has now taken place no more than four years after the billing periods in question commenced. Why did the Pure Leisure Group (P.L.G.) have to have one?

It is nearly three years since I first wrote to P.L.G. on the 20th October 2008 querying the 76.5% increase in the electric charges. Despite numerous and constant letters from me it took P.L.G. nearly two years to acknowledge my concerns and this I believe only took place because I had brought in solicitors to act for me, whereby, through the law, you are bound to respond, which you eventually did.

I don't know whether you have read the complete file from the commencement of my actions but it is clear for all to see that P.L.G. has acted in a totally disgraceful manner and particularly by its refusal to even acknowledge my correspondance. I suspect those 'handling' the matter did not have the answer. This a wretched, long drawn-out saga ensued.

Despite the massive, comprehensive reply by yourself, which took from the 6th July

1

107

2010 to the 7th March 2011 to produce, I believe P.L.G. and the suppliers, Energy Cost Management (E.C.M.) have formed a 'cahoots' situation to protect each others interests and figures (eg spread sheets) you have produced have been manipulated, even invented?

You may feel free to proceed in seeking the recovery of the substantial 'undercharge.' In my case it comes to £15.94 + V.A.T.

You state that the maintanance charges are included in the unit prices shown. Ofgen's ruling is that these charges must be billed separately, therefore your invoices are technically illegal and unenforceable.

You have now just created and produced figures in an attempt to justify your charging methods, but why _years_ later?

Correspondence from E.C.M. to the writer proves beyond doubt that P.L.G. deliberately brought forward the annual pence per unit price by one year for each of the three years in question (plus year ending 2010?)

The following is a quote from E.C.M's letter dated 6th July 2009 :- "We do not get involved with the re-charging that Pure Leisure does for their customers. You may wish to contact them direct."

Electric costs at my Preston address per unit from the 19th February 2010 to the 24th November 2010 were, secondary 9.030p and primary, 14.054p written proof is available.

I requested to pay my pitch fees by installments as I did not wish to pay out a full years site fees _in advance_ whilst residing there under a 'dark cloud '.

You state P.L.G. pay their electric bills monthly but recover these yearly in arrear. On this theme I note, P.L,G.' s residents have to pay their site fees one year in advance and the site fee deposit (£500.00) seventeen months in advance.

I am aware of a great number of residents who complain about the electric charges but do not wish to get involved especially in a area where their purpose is to be relaxed and free from hassle.

E.C.M., in their letter of the 20th April 2010, state that they could not enter into any further correspondence or discussions with me as instructed by P.L.G. and that the file had been closed.

It is noted that touring caravans on your parks were charged, during the years in question, the same unit rate as the static caravans even though on average they spend far less time in residence.

Would you kindly confirm the unit rate you have charged in respect of all your other caravan parks during the years in question. I will need this information for the new

2

government advocacy body, Comsumer Focus, who advise the Office of Fair Trading.

I will be presenting them with the complete file, including this letter and also to Ofgem. I understand P.L.G. cater for several thousand units, including over two thousand at one park only.

In the absence of any reply to this letter (which is expected) I will be in communications with the fore mentioned bodies during the early course of November 2011.

To get to the bottom of this matter, I believe a vigorous, in-depth and internal investigation/audit of P.L.G.'s and E.C.M.'s records and accounts by Consumer Focus has to take place.

Yours Truly,

Septimus Cooper

11th November 2011

Recorded Delivery
Private and Confidential
Without Prejudice
For the attention of Mr C. Royle
Group Solicitor and Company Secretary

Pure Leisure Group   1 St. Anthony's Close
South Lakeland House   Milnthorpe
Yealand Redmayne   Cumbria
Carnforth   LA7 7DT
Lancashire
LA5 9RN

Dear Mr Royle,   **Re-Electricity Charges**
                                    255 Fell End Caravan Park

With reference to my recorded delivery letter of the 13th October 2011 (to which a reply has not been received), I have been advised due to my age, health problems and other factors to try and bring a cessation to this long drawn –out sordid saga.

In this light I would refer you to your incorrectly dated letter i.e. 7th February 2010 and posted on the 7th March 2011 in which you offered a sum of £1,079.97 provided I would cease with my claim against you. I am prepared to accept a figure satisfactory to me which would have to take into account my expenses, time spent stress, worry etc. over the three year period and caused also by the eviction.

The actions I intend to take, as outlined in my earlier letter, will commence unless you reply by 26th November 2011, this could also include a National Sunday/Daily paper being brought into the proceedings.

Yours Truly,

Septimus Cooper

pure leisure
UK & INTERNATIONAL HOLIDAY

Mr S Cooper
1 St Anthony's Close
Milnthorpe
Cumbria
LA7 7DT

21st November 2011

Dear Mr Cooper

Electricity charges 255 Fell End Caravan Park

In reply to your letter dated 11th November the offer to settle your electricity claim was made as part of the deal for buying in your caravan. You declined that part of the offer and the same is no longer on the table and open for acceptance. In any event the time limit for accepting the offer has long since expired.

So far as we are concerned the matter is now closed

Yours faithfully

Chris Royle

Group Solicitor & Company Secretary

PURE LEISURE GROUP

South Lakeland House
Yealand Redmayne, Carnforth
Lancashire. LA5 9RN UK.

t: +44 (0) 1524 781918
f: +44 (0) 1524 782243
e: enquiries@pureleisuregroup

APPENDIX R

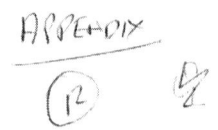

1st December 2011
C Royle Esq.
Group Solicitor and Company Secretary
Pure Leisure Group
South Lakeland House
Yealand Redmayne
Carnforth
Lancashire
LA5 9RN

1 St. Anthony's Close
Milnthorpe
Cumbria
LA7 7DT

Dear Mr Royle,

Re- Electricity Charges -255 Fell End Caravan Park

I refer to your letter of the 21st November 2011.

I am at a loss when you state that the offer to settle my electricity claim "was made as part of the deal for buying in the caravan" this is just not true and I would refer to your letter dated 7th February 2010." to my solicitors in which you state and again I quote " we offered to waive the outstanding electricity charges......provided that your client would agree to cease his claim against us …. please note the offer is made with a view to disposing of the claim."

I am now commencing actions as previously outlined which will also include your company's wrongful eviction process and possible court proceedings.

Yours truly,

Septimus Cooper

18. THE EVICTION – AND ITS CONSEQUENCES

We all hope the New Year will bring better fortune. In spite of this possibility I was also aware that as at this New Year's Day Mr. Royle's last communication was dated the 4th October 2010 I was in a frame of mind which wasn't conducive to giving out verbal "all the best" messages. Being totally unfair, I suppose, to all those around me.

On this day, I wrote in confidence to the Park Manager, a Mr. John Hurst, whom I got on quite well with. I was aware of course that he was the son-in-law of Mr. J. Morphet, the chairman and owner of the Pure Leisure Group. This alternative course of action, born out of desperation, proved once again my naïvety. It also resulted finally in my complete lack of trust with all and sundry employed at the Fell End Park. At the time I was thinking there must be at least one good apple in the management barrel.

My letter to Mr. Hurst in essence stated the following: "I had taken him into my confidence regarding the electric fraud situation which was in the hands of my solicitors but the scenario now covered 2008/09/10/11. I liked living on the park but being under and within a cloud of mistrust was getting me down". He kindly agreed at a meeting on the 8th of January to speak to his father-in-law and would come back to me by the 16th. He didn't, but was now having a further meeting with his father-in-law on the 17th. Again this proved negative so I wrote to him on the 25th. He verbally replied he was having a further meeting on the 28th. All to no avail I'm afraid. Adding salt to the wound Mr. Hurst had in fact handed my letter over to Mr. Royle, which was confirmed in the latter's letter to me of the 14th February 2011.

I will return to Mr. Hurst a little later in the book when his actions inspired a feeling of disgust within me. At this stage of my writings I don't wish to sound overdramatic but I would like to point out that parts of the following passages do not make for easy reading.

The park closes for static caravans each year for six weeks. My wife and I normally rented a cottage in the Lake District for this closure period, mid-January to the end of February, however we chose the nearby village of Milnthorpe for our accommodation. Due to medical reasons I could no longer drive. On the 16th February 2011 our son happened to call on us. He was on business but agreed to my request to call at Fell End. He duly collected the mail and on checking over the caravan came across an A4 size, encapsulated, undated notice. It was in large lettering and sellotaped to the window on the door. It is reproduced herein (reference two). Please take your time in trying to grasp the enormity of its consequences on our lives. When my son telephoned me initially he just couldn't bring himself to give me the news. Now I ask you, my loyal readers, to put yourselves into the position my wife and I found ourselves in. In particular you Mothers and Wives. The Fell End management knew it was our permanent home. We had barely two weeks to re-arrange our future (and at my age of seventy). The principle of these indescribable actions is just the same as if a house was involved. Fell End had on record my contact telephone number while I was away.

Then fate, or a *saint*, intervened and played a hand. I realised all my efforts must now be concentrated on finding a place to live. Time was of the essence. If necessary I had to rely on friends or Stagecoach for getting about. My agenda included solicitors, estate agents, property owners and referees. Indeed, all those institutions who have always given me the impression that time was unimportant. Regarding references what would I do if it was insisted I provide one from my latest landlord, i.e. Fell End? With under two weeks left on my temporary tenancy the position appeared hopeless. My determination not to impose myself on "family" however remained steadfast. B&B? Hotel? Y.H.A.? Storage?

The day after my son brought home the eviction notices (which included one in my 'mail box') I went as usual into the village for the daily paper. The newsagent had a noticeboard outside where one could, within reason, advertise almost anything. I gave it slightly more than my usual cursory glance. Well, one never knows – but there it was in all its glory – to me anyway. To let, 1 *Saint* Anthony's Close. Door to door not forty yards away from our temporary accommodation. Margaret and I had admired this property for some time. Well, the "if only" thoughts were to become a reality. Surprisingly, there was no indication that it was to let. Within three days, the owner was provided with an impeccable reference from a prominent Lake District solicitor. This was followed with a firm promise of two more. One from a well-known, old, established, family-owned South Lakeland estate agent, the third being a top city accountant.

One month's rent in advance together with the necessary bond was offered after viewing. Our new landlord then said that a reference from Fell End Park would no longer be necessary. On the first of March we moved in. We were once again "urbanites", but that's another story. We are still here over four years later. As Margaret later reflected – "if we don't move again you can't make a wrong move again". After what she had experienced (which I will now briefly explain) I let her words of wisdom pass over my head.

We now had a place to live and despite being blessed with a stoic nature my wife's nervous system, quite understandably, had reached a low point. Fortunately our daughter and her family lived in the idyllic Greek village of Afitos. It was situated on the edge of the Aegean Sea. From there, she rang me regularly and in time sounded relaxed and happy.

Now I move away from the silver lining of this episode and back into the dark, sombre clouds and aftermath of the Fell End Park horror show. Rule 18.2 of the park's licence conditions and site rules states: "The company reserves the right to terminate a licence to occupy a pitch as a consequence of a serious breach of agreement that is not capable of remedy by the holiday home owner upon serving reasonable written notice at the last known address of the occupier to that effect specifying the breach and the occupier's rights in relation thereto". My comments regarding this ruling are as follows although I know you will have, in the main, cottoned on to what I am about to say.

1. For my part there was no breach of any description whatsoever, therefore I could not remedy something which did not exist.

2. The eviction notice did not specify in any way what breach of the agreement had been committed.
3. In all, was the written (eviction) notice "reasonable"?
4. Their rules and regulations nowhere state the company's entitlement to disconnect the "electrical, gas and water supply".
5. Again there rules do not include, contrary to the threats made to me by Messrs Green and Crowe via Mr. Hurst the following: unless a buy-back was agreed I would be liable to pay £50.00 per day storage charges in effect from the commencement of the new season (i.e. the 1st March 2011). In addition to this £500.00 plus V.A.T. would be charged, again for "storage" for the six weeks when the park was closed. They were setting out their stall for the kill.
6. Within the company's rules and regulations you will observe herein that the homeowner must give two months notice in writing. The company however need only give one month. I wasn't even given one second.

Whilst I am no mind reader, I initially believed that in their twisted pride, the build-up of frustration and anger, all logic went clean out of the window. They in fact lost control of their senses. Subconsciously they were cleansing their greed-filled minds from the accumulation of gremlins therein. They snapped and plunged recklessly onto my abode. Support for this manoeuvre would also arise from their foolish belief that whatever wrongful acts they perpetrated on the park they were immune from the law as we know it. After all 'Big Brothers'' site rules and regulations saw to this. Didn't they?

In giving the matter further thought however, and in particular with regard to the explanations given for the Fell End Park's management's actions, it dawned on me I could have got it all wrong. Perhaps it was all just to do with their normal cold-blooded, ruthless, run of the mill company policy. I would be more than interested to see the result of a reader's ballot on this!

Some weeks after discovering the eviction notice I wrote to Mr. Hurst (reference three) pointing out that according to Mr. David Griffiths, a park employee, he had under your instructions helped in the carrying-out of the eviction process. Although he replied, his poorly spelt letter of the 6th April (reference four - enclosed) was one of total denial in respect of his involvement. I wrote to him again on the 13th April (reference five) with a few poignant questions. No reply was forthcoming. In a further letter of the 10th May I wrote: "I have written evidence that you personally played a part in the eviction process." Again, no reply. Herein and following this page you will also find enclosed the following in confirmation of the foregoing:

1. Mr Hurst's handwritten addressed envelope (copy) which contained the eviction notice
2. A copy of the eviction notice left in my mailbox
3. A copy of my letter to Mr. Hurst on 30.03.2011
4. A copy of Mr Hurst's reply of 06.04.2011
5. My reply to this of 13.04.2011
6, 7, 8. A letter, a court witness statement and a statement of truth from Elaine Quigley B.A. Hons, F.B.I.G. (Dip) fellow of the British institute of Graphologists. Therein you will observe the highest category (out of five) of certainty possible is appropriate, i.e. proving 1. and 4. are both written by Mr. Hurst.

I found this dramatic, incontestable highest possible professional evidence unsurprising. To me it exemplified the level of depravity Fell End Park's management were capable of. A wickedness I was having to continually bear. A pressure I have to admit not carried without great restraint and a weight my old shoulders had to continue to persevere with.

Mr Cooper 255
% Fell End Caravan Park

NOTICE OF TERMINATION OF RIGHT TO SITE A CARAVAN HOLIDAY HOME AT FELLEND CARAVAN PARK.

IMMEDIATE ACTION REQUIRED PLEASE CALL 01524 784784 ASK FOR ANDY CROWE THIS CARAVAN HAS BEEN DISCONECTED FROM THE ELECTRICAL, GAS AND WATER SUPPLY

30.03.11

No. 1, St. Anthony's Close,
Milnthorpe,
Cumbria.
LA7 7DT

(3)

Dear John,   RE. 255, FELL END CARAVAN PARK —
             THE EVICTION.

Shortly after we discovered the eviction notice on the caravan door together with the severed electric cable, disconnected gas pipes, etc., (which David your groundsman stated he had carried out under your instructions) we also discovered, when moving out, that of the three gas bottles we had, there was only one remaining. Of the two missing one was full.

We wondered if you could enlighten us as to their disappearance. Perhaps they were taken by mistake as part of the eviction process.

In view of our (enforced) new address kindly find enclosed stamped addressed envelope.

Thanking you in anticipation of your reply in early course.

Yours Sincerely

(SEPTIMUS COUPER)

— To —
John Hirst Esq.,
The Park Manager,
Fell End Caravan Park,
Hale,
Milnthorpe,
Cumbria.   LA7 7BS

'Silent' copy to
Ratcliffe & Bibby
Solicitors. ✓

6/4/11 (R) 4/4/11 (4)   Fell End Caravan
                           Slackhead Rd
                           Hale
Hello Sept   Nr Milnthorp
                           Cumbria
                           LA77BS

    As you are aware I was away on holiday in February, and when I returned I was told that you where Leaving the Park and you had agreed to sell your caravan pa'

    As far as I was aware it had all been carried out Amicabally between you and Andy Crowe,

    I new nothing about an Evicti or did I instruct David to Sever the Electric cable ETC,

    I saw Johnno and asked about your well being and he said you were fi and happy with your move, I hope this clears up the matter, and I wish you well for the future,

    Thanks

    John Hurst

12.04.11

1, Strathways Close,
Milnthorpe,
Cumbria
LA7 7DT

Dear John,

Thank you for your letter of the 6th April 2011.

I am sorry. I thought you (as Park Manager) would have been the one to instruct David to carry out "the decommissioning" so that I may set my facts right in any future correspondence. Would you kindly (1) confirm when you recommenced your duties. Also, I would be very grateful if you would (2) liaise with David as to the name of the P.L.S. employee who gave him his instructions.

John has stated to me that it appears you had misread his reply as to you asking about my well-being (for which I thank you). He did in fact state I was happy in our new abode and ammenities in Milnthorpe. What he did not mention was our distress at being evicted from the Park. It's a long story which will continue. My wife became ill and depressed, for example.

Thanking you very much in paticipation of your reply and answers to the two questions raised.

Yours sincerely,

(Septimus Cooper)

-To-
Mr John Hurst.
Park Manager,
Fell End Caravan Park
Hale
LA7 7BS

Elaine Quigley B.A. Hons. F.B.I.G. (Dip) Graphologist
Fellow and Past Chairman of The British Institute of Graphologists

LANGDALE HOUSE, 7 HILL RISE CRESCENT, CHALFONT ST PETER, BUCKS, SL9 9BW

01753 886412 elainequigley@sky.com www.britishgraphology.org

Mr Septimus Cooper 17th July 2014
No. 1. St Anthony's Close
Milnthorpe
Cumbria, LA7 7DT

Dear Mr Cooper

Re your request for document examination

I have examined and compared the sample letter and the writing on the envelope and I am fairly sure that they are by the same hand.

An acetate copy was made of the writing on the envelope and the letters on this were placed over similar letters on the letter signed John Hurst.

There were several that matched very closely and there were idiosyncrasies in the letter shapes that reinforced my judgement that the two pieces of writing are by the same person.

If you wish me to proceed with an official Court Ready report, please let me know. The cost for this can be £50, which is well below my usual rcharge of £100, but I am prepared to reduce the fee, as the job has been straightforward.

If you decide to take this further, please send a cheque for £50 made payable to me and I will produce a full document that is acceptable to the Court.

Yours sincerely

Elaine Quigley

Mrs Elaine Quigley

Elaine Quigley B.A. Hons. F.B.I.G. (Dip)
FELLOW OF THE BRITISH INSTITUTE OF GRAPHOLOGISTS
Graphologist and Document Examiner

Witness Statement of Elaine Quigley, B.A. Hons, F.B.I.G. (Dip)

I, Elaine Quigley,
of Langdale House, Hill Rise Crescent, Chalfont St Peter, Bucks, SL9 9BW, state as follows.

QUALIFICATIONS, BACKGROUND AND EXPERIENCE

The British Institute of Graphologist diploma - January 1991
Since then, document examination of samples of writing and numbers, over a range of languages.
Expert witness retained by solicitors for defendant and plaintiff jointly.
Examination of malicious correspondence.
Examination of historical documents to identify or verify the writer.
Identification of the true writers in a high-profile 19th Century case.
Expert witness at Dublin Four Courts in a successful Defamation of Character case.

Re comparison of Signatures on financial documents

INSTRUCTIONS

A request has been made to me by **Mr Septimus Cooper** of No.1 St Anthony's Close, Milnthorp. Cumbria, LA7 7DT, to compare the writing on a letter from John Hurst (**Specimen 1**), with writing on an envelope, (**Specimen 2**)- copies of which will be included in this report.

DOCUMENTS FOR COMPARISON

Both these documents are original copies, and an acetate template has been made of the writing on the envelope (Specimen 2), so that it can be superimposed on the letter from John Hurst, Specimen 1, to double check the closeness of the match between the two.

METHODOLOGY

Examination under magnification has been undertaken to identify the small details of certain letters and a report on findings is given below.

Mr Cooper 255
℅ Fell End Caravan Park

Specimen 2 - Envelope

The Acetate sheet copied from the envelope was carefully laid on all letters that were available to compare with those on the main letter signed John Hurst.

1. The slant and dimensions match those on the Hurst letter very closely.

2. The letter 'r' in 'Mr' is replicated many times in the Hurst letter.

3. The letters 'C,c' on the envelope are made and slanted the same way as those in the letter.

4. The letter 'o', though knotted on the envelope version, on the letter it slants at the same angle and is mostly the same size.

5. The letter 'e' in 'Cooper' and 'Fell' is very much the same size and with the same connective formation as the 'e's in the Hurst letter.

6. The letter 'a' seen twice on the envelope is a very close match throughout the Hurst letter.

7. The letter 'd' in 'End' on the envelope has a shorter stem than the letters 'd' in the Hurst letter, but the style and structure are the same.

8. The upper case 'P' seen in the word 'Park' on the envelope has an unusual movement as the circle joins the stem. This is repeated in the same letter 'P' in the word 'Park' in the address, top right corner and 'Park' at the start of the 4th line down, both in the Hurst letter.

9. With this amount of evidence, given the size and slant match and the number of letters that match in the way they are constructed, in my professional opinion, I believe that category No. 5, Highly Possible, is appropriate.

Categories of Certainty

1. Inconclusive: Too little or inferior material is available for comparison.
2. Unlikely: Too many differences.
3. Possible: Some resemblances, but differences as well.
4. Probable: A preponderance of probabilities over possibilities seems to be a reasonable conclusion.
5. Highly possible: Near certain

Duty to the Court

I understand my duty to the Court is to assist the Court with matters within my expertise and I have complied with that duty.

I understand that this duty overrides any obligations to those by whom I have been instructed or by whom I am paid.

I believe that I have taken into account the range of expert opinions in relation to matter set out in this report.

The reasons for reaching my conclusion are set out in the body of this report.

STATEMENT OF TRUTH

I confirm that insofar as the facts stated in my report are within my own knowledge I have made clear which they are and I believe them to be true and that the opinions I have expressed represent my true and complete professional opinion.

Signed: *Elaine Quigley* 28th July 2014
Elaine Quigley

Then came the erection of yellow tape which surrounded my caravan. This indicated a possible crime scene scenario or, forsooth a "danger – keep out" zone. This action was disclosed to me by a resident of long-standing and still on the park. As far as he knew it was "a first". For one reason or another numerous static caravans are vacated and become permanently unoccupied every year. Why accentuate *my* departure, creating a focal point? You may or may not agree but I suggest their management had a school of thought which was one of:

1. "We'll show the Park and all therein who's the boss"
2. "Nobody does wrong by us, especially Cooper"
3. Highlighting my past home's presence to aid a sale!

Are there any other theories out there?

I now turn to my sale and buy-back experience. It's my turn now, I'm afraid.

Many, many hours were spent in changing a wilderness into a large, beautiful woodland garden. Two years after the commencement of my landscaping efforts, and indeed those of my teenage grand-daughter, the completed article had no parallel on the park. The improvements included the introduction of lawns, rockeries and paths which intertwined with numerous and varied shrubs, plants and flowers (some wild). We had all-round wooden skirting installed. A large decking area measuring 25' by 8', we had the home fitted with Venetian blinds throughout which were made to order by a well-known local tradesman. Underneath was insulated with panels, and a large concrete-based shed rounded it all off. May I put it this way? I was extremely proud of the improvements!

In observing the brutal statistics from the following analysis you may find that, like me, they do take some digesting. They are all supported, I once again reiterate, by written evidence.

2005 Cost of new home: £39,000
2011 Buy-back of home: £13,000
6 Year Loss: £26,000
6 Year cost of rents/rates: £15,814
6 Year Cost Total: £41,814
6 year x 46 week season on park equates to 276 weeks at **£151.50 per week =** £41,814
£00,000

Note: electric/gas weekly costs not included

Unlike the great majority of holiday home owners no other weekly home overheads had to be found, however this was to a large degree offset by the appreciation in value of the house I had sold six years earlier. This turned out to be in the region of £30,000 (thirty thousand pounds), or £100.00 per week.

The cost of renting a house on six occasions (whilst the six week 'off-park' ruling was in force' amounted to £5,400 (five-thousand four hundred pounds).

Finally on this subject I fast forward to my solicitor's letter to Pure Leisure of the 3rd May 2012: "…with respect to his eviction from the site and the manner in which you acquired his caravan… your strategy appears to have been to invent a level of indebtedness which did not in reality exist with a view to evicting our client and acquiring his property for a fraction of its true value… we believe that a court will be sympathetic to our client's claim for damages based on the losses incurred through the sale of his caravan under duress".

INTERLUDE – PAUSE FOR THOUGHT

At times when writing this book I have had to stop prior to my intended stint, usually to take a walk. Sometimes I soon return to recommence putting pen to paper – sometimes not – the former only takes place when I have got rid of the ire, the mental ache and the pent-up feelings of frustration, these all brought on by what I am compelled to write knowing the subject of which sorely blemishes the lives of hard-working honest folk who are, ironically, just looking for a getaway from a world full of these very pressures!

19. THE ELECTRICITY FRAUD PART TWO

As stated earlier, I now return to a further part reluctantly played in this story by Energy Cost Management Ltd. (E.C.M.). I say reluctantly because they have been asked by the Pure Leisure Group Ltd. (*not* Pure Leisure) to distort the truth; being under what may be described as an enforced obligation to probably one of their most important customers. An "in cahoots" situation developed. This was inevitable. Indeed, later in the book you will observe my solicitor asserting that E.C.M. are in fact agents of P.L.G. although this was strenuously denied by Mr. Royle. It was not denied or even mentioned in E.C.M.'s letter to me of the 10th April 2012. This letter was in reply to a letter of mine dated the 4th April 2012, in which I referred to them as agents of P.L.G.. However, moving on enclosed herein are copies of letters from E.C.M. and the P.L.G. dated 20th September 2010 (reference one) and the 4th October 2010 (reference two) respectively. Also enclosed herein is a mass of statistics involving figures, dates, items etc. (reference three) provided by E.C.M. for P.L.G.. These, you will have noted, are proudly referred to by Mr. Royle as "the spread sheet". Unfortunately, this extensive and bold attempt to justify the rates that had been charged (over a three year period) included the costs of maintenance etc.. Totally illegal and indeed fraudulent. Kindly bear with me. All will be revealed later on in the book. On the face of it the spreadsheet, together with E.C.M.'s letter, dovetailed perfectly for P.L.G.'s needs of escape. In connection with E.C.M.'s letter (reference two) I would ask the following question: What have the running costs to do with E.C.M.? Surely their sole job is to provide electricity at the best possible rate and that's it. From the start their exercise in producing figures to suit was pointless. Five words from their letter - "based on the information provided" (I guess by no less than 'honest joe' Royle himself) speaks volumes. In addition you will note E.C.M.'s letter includes innuendos such as 'there would appear' and 'we estimate'. No concrete, neutral facts whatsoever. How could there be?

To me, the contents of E.C.M.'s written reply are a fabrication of the truth borne out of collusion with the Pure Leisure group, the master of the situation. With nerves probably playing a part E.C.M. calculated the V.A.T. rate (year 2007) at 7%. Firm endorsement of the facts and figures distortion is highlighted by the following analysis.

Year	Contract Price (fact)	E.C.M.	P.L.G (fact)
2007	7.06	"undercharged by £11,600"	7.06
2008	7.06	12.63	12.63
2009	12.63	14.04	13.39
2010	12.63	-	15.26

By now I'm sure you will be asking yourselves the question – "what on earth is going on?". As and if you proceed reading my story it will tell you. If you eventually accept what I still to this day believe P.L.G. were up to then this book will to a great degree have served its purpose.

Reference One

ENERGY COST MANAGEMENT · E C M ·

SDC/SHC

20th September 2010

Mr A Green
Operations Director
Pure Leisure Group
South Lakeland House
Yealand
Carnforth
Lancashire
LA5 9RN

Dear Alan

Fell End Caravan Park
Electricity Re-Charges

Further to our recent meeting and our review of the electricity charges we are now able to offer the following:

Our review has covered the utility billing periods June 2006 to August 2009. We would advise that there would appear to be a number of under-charges, one of which may pre-dates the periods where charges have been queried.

Based on the information provided we estimate that the under-charge for the period June 2006 to July 2007 is ~£11,600. Further information would be required to determine how long this undercharge has occurred but would be limited by the Statute of Limitations.

With regard to the period August 2007 to September 2008 we would confirm that the re-charge rate of 12.63p/kWh accurately reflects the charges and costs incurred.

With regard to the charging period August 2008-Aug 2009, we note that no repair costs were included. Also the rate charged of 14.06p/kWh should have been 14.04p/kWh plus VAT.

We would advise that we have not received details of costs associated with Repairs to Service and which may constitute an undercharge.

Energy Cost Management Ltd, The Old Printworks, Birley Street, Kirkham, Preston PR4 2AT
telephone: 01772 682323   facsimile: 01772 686080   solutions@ecm-uk.com   www.ecm-uk.com
registered in england and wales, company reg no. 3527052   vat no 693287393

YOUR PARTNER IN UTILITY COST REDUCTION

·ECM·

We would suggest that the meter reading, administration and site charge, taking into account your credit facility made available for the unit owners, is perhaps a little on the low side and could be reviewed.

The attached summary is enclosed for your review and which we trust meets with your approval. In the meantime should you have any queries please do not hesitate to contact me.

Yours sincerely

Steve Casson

Enc

Reference Two

Mr J Tomlinson

Messrs Ratcliffe & Bibby

Castle Chambers 60 Market Street

Lancaster LA1 1HP

4th October 2010

Your ref JT/JT/COO1871/I

Dear Mr Tomlinson

Complaint re electricity charges your client Mr S Cooper

I am now in a position to reply to your letter of 26th July last and I apologise for the long delay in so doing

First of all I have to point out to you and your client that although a resupplier of electricity is not allowed to make a profit on the resale price of electricity, it is lawful for it to recover from its unit owners a proportion of the standing charge and also its associated and relative costs incurred in connection with the resupply of electricity. This consists of the cost of metering, meter reading administration and costs, repairs and renewals to the system, and credit charges. We pay the electricity bills monthly but only recover these from our customers yearly in arrear.

Our energy costs consultants Energy Cost Management Ltd have undertaken a comprehensive review of our recharging rates and we think that we can do no better than send to you herewith a copy of their letter to us dated 20th September last and the spread sheet accompanying the same.

It will no doubt not have escaped your notice that for the year 2006 – 07 there has been a substantial undercharge to unit owners and for 2008 – 09 the rate charged should have been 14.11p per unit and not 14.06p.

We trust that the foregoing will satisfy your client and no further action will be taken by him in which case we will not address the issue of undercharging nor seek to recover the same from your client accordingly.

Yours sincerely

Chris Royle

Group Solicitor and Company Secretary

Reference Three

Site: Fell End Caravan Park
Type: Electricity
Number: 00845251 1600000170830

£360.00   £36.00   £4,900.00

Associated Electricity Supply On Costs **ACE**

Billing period	Date	E	kWh	Cost £ inc VAT	Cost £ Exc VAT	Invoice Monthly average price exc. VAT	Code 5 Metering cost	Meter Reading and admin at site	Repairs & Renewals to Service	Total Monthly costs	Total Average price per month	PLG rate of charge inc VAT
1	30/06/2006	N	24983	£1,944.96	£1,852.34	7.41	£30.00	£660.00	£350.00	£2,892.34	11.58	
2	31/07/2006	N	24687	£1,929.21	£1,837.34	7.44	£30.00	£660.00	£350.00	£2,877.34	11.66	
3	31/08/2006	N	29721	£2,275.73	£2,167.36	7.29	£30.00	£660.00	£350.00	£3,207.30	10.79	
4	30/09/2006	N	26808	£2,087.72	£1,989.26	7.40	£30.00	£660.00	£350.00	£3,009.26	11.31	
5	31/10/2006	N	39430	£2,931.27	£2,791.69	7.08	£30.00	£660.00	£350.00	£3,831.69	9.72	
6	30/11/2006	N	48718	£3,587.75	£3,416.90	6.87	£30.00	£660.00	£350.00	£4,456.90	8.96	
7	31/12/2006	N	52218	£3,750.23	£3,571.65	6.84	£30.00	£660.00	£350.00	£4,611.85	8.83	2.06 + VAT = 2.55
8	31/01/2007	N	37359	£2,747.12	£2,616.30	7.00	£30.00	£660.00	£350.00	£3,656.30	9.79	
9 & 10	31/03/2007	N	53007	£3,794.37	£3,613.64	6.82	£30.00	£660.00	£350.00	£4,653.64	8.78	
11	30/04/2007	N	44369	£3,211.29	£3,058.37	6.89	£30.00	£660.00	£350.00	£4,098.37	9.24	
12	31/05/2007	N	37667	£2,805.13	£2,671.55	7.09	£30.00	£660.00	£350.00	£3,711.55	9.85	
13	30/06/2007	N	25833	£2,015.29	£1,919.32	7.43	£30.00	£660.00	£350.00	£2,959.32	11.45	
14	31/07/2007	N	27119	£2,117.26	£2,016.44	7.44	£30.00	£660.00	£350.00	£3,056.44	11.27	
						8.64		Average price including uplift			9.52	7.20
			472719									

£360.00   £36.00   £12,200.00

1	31/08/2007	N	31794	£2,432.77	£2,316.92	7.29	£30.00	£660.00	£871.43	£3,878.35	12.20	
2	30/09/2007	N	31734	£2,426.29	£2,310.67	7.28	£30.00	£660.00	£871.43	£3,872.10	12.20	
3	31/10/2007	N	43841	£3,222.01	£3,068.58	7.00	£30.00	£660.00	£871.43	£4,630.01	10.56	
4	30/11/2007	N	50696	£3,679.40	£3,504.19	6.91	£30.00	£660.00	£871.43	£5,065.62	9.98	
5	31/12/2007	N	57138	£4,706.39	£4,482.28	7.84	£30.00	£660.00	£871.43	£6,043.70	10.58	
6	31/01/2008	N	39562	£3,325.43	£3,167.08	8.01	£30.00	£660.00	£871.43	£4,728.50	11.95	
7	29/02/2008	N	30130	£2,583.84	£2,460.80	8.17	£30.00	£660.00	£871.43	£4,022.23	13.35	12.63 + VAT = 13.76
8	31/03/2008	N	60699	£4,956.19	£4,720.18	7.78	£30.00	£660.00	£871.43	£6,281.61	10.35	
9	30/04/2008	N	48823	£4,046.02	£3,853.36	7.89	£30.00	£660.00	£871.43	£5,414.79	11.09	
10	31/05/2008	N	34244	£2,959.85	£2,818.90	8.23	£30.00	£660.00	£871.43	£4,380.33	12.79	
11	30/06/2008	N	29889	£2,636.19	£2,510.66	8.40	£30.00	£660.00	£871.43	£4,072.09	13.62	
12	31/07/2008	N	27506	£2,453.87	£2,337.02	8.50	£30.00	£660.00	£871.43	£3,898.45	14.17	
13	31/08/2008	N	32262	£3,977.10	£3,787.71	11.74	£30.00	£660.00	£871.43	£5,349.14	16.58	
14	30/09/2008	N	32610	£4,312.27	£4,106.92	12.59	£30.00	£660.00	£871.43	£5,668.35	17.38	
						8.47		Average price including uplift			12.631	12.63

£360.00   £36.00   £0.00

1	31/10/2008	N	48152	£5,951.71	£5,668.30	11.77	£30.00	£660.00	£0.00	£6,358.30	13.20	
2	30/11/2008	N	47610	£5,861.27	£5,582.16	11.72	£30.00	£660.00	£0.00	£6,272.16	13.17	
3	31/12/2008	M	54474	£6,643.04	£6,326.70	11.61	£30.00	£660.00	£0.00	£7,016.70	12.88	
4	31/01/2009	N	41684	£6,147.04	£4,901.94	11.79	£30.00	£660.00	£0.00	£5,591.94	13.45	
5	28/02/2009	N	30142	£3,831.52	£3,649.07	12.11	£30.00	£660.00	£0.00	£4,339.07	14.40	13.38 + VAT = 14.06
6	31/03/2009	N	40831	£5,087.34	£4,845.09	11.84	£30.00	£660.00	£0.00	£5,535.09	13.52	
7	30/04/2009	N	39688	£4,921.83	£4,687.27	11.81	£30.00	£660.00	£0.00	£5,377.27	13.55	
8	31/05/2009	N	33725	£4,268.95	£4,065.67	12.06	£30.00	£660.00	£0.00	£4,755.67	14.10	
9	30/06/2009	N	22772	£3,004.06	£2,861.03	12.56	£30.00	£660.00	£0.00	£3,551.03	15.59	
10	31/07/2009	N	22541	£2,990.23	£2,847.84	12.63	£30.00	£660.00	£0.00	£3,537.84	15.70	
11	31/08/2009	N	27515	£3,577.74	£3,407.37	12.38	£30.00	£660.00	£0.00	£4,097.37	14.89	
						12.03		Average price including uplift			14.04	14.06

Site: Fell End Caravan Park
Type: Electricity
Number: 00845251 1600000170830

£360.00   £36.00   £4,900.00

Associated Electricity Supply On Costs

Billing period	Date	E	kWh	Cost £ inc VAT	Cost £ Exc VAT	Invoice Monthly average price exc. VAT	Code 5 Metering cost	Meter Reading and admin at site	Repairs & Renewals to Service	Total Monthly costs	Total Average price per month	PLG rate of charge exc VAT
1	30/06/2006	N	24983	£1,944.96	£1,852.34	7.41	£30.00	£660.00	£350.00	£2,892.34	11.58	
2	31/07/2006	N	24687	£1,929.21	£1,837.34	7.44	£30.00	£660.00	£350.00	£2,877.34	11.66	
3	31/08/2006	N	29721	£2,275.73	£2,157.36	7.29	£30.00	£660.98	£350.00	£3,207.36	12.79	
4	30/09/2006	N	26808	£2,067.72	£1,968.26	7.40	£30.00	£660.00	£350.00	£3,009.26	11.31	
5	31/10/2006	N	39430	£2,931.27	£2,791.59	7.08	£30.00	£660.00	£350.00	£3,831.59	9.72	
6	30/11/2006	N	49718	£3,587.75	£3,416.90	6.87	£30.00	£660.00	£350.00	£4,456.90	8.96	
7	31/12/2006	N	52218	£3,750.23	£3,571.65	6.84	£30.00	£660.00	£350.00	£4,611.65	8.83	7.06 + VAT
8	31/01/2007	N	37350	£2,747.12	£2,616.30	7.00	£30.00	£660.00	£350.00	£3,656.30	8.78	= 7.55
9 & 10	31/03/2007	N	53007	£3,794.32	£3,613.64	6.82	£30.00	£660.00	£350.00	£4,653.64	8.78	
11	30/04/2007	N	44369	£3,211.29	£3,058.37	6.89	£30.00	£660.00	£350.00	£4,098.37	9.24	
12	31/05/2007	N	37667	£2,905.13	£2,871.55	7.09	£30.00	£660.00	£350.00	£3,711.55	9.85	
13	30/06/2007	N	25833	£2,015.29	£1,919.32	7.43	£30.00	£660.00	£350.00	£2,959.32	11.46	
14	31/07/2007	N	27119	£2,117.26	£2,016.44	7.44	£30.00	£660.00	£350.00	£3,056.44	11.27	
						5.64			Average price including uplift		9.52	7.96

427719

£360.00   £36.00   £12,200.00

1	31/08/2007	N	31794	£2,432.77	£2,318.92	7.28	£30.00	£660.00	£871.43	£3,878.35	12.20	
2	30/09/2007	N	31734	£2,426.20	£2,310.67	7.28	£30.00	£660.00	£871.43	£3,872.10	12.20	
3	31/10/2007	N	43841	£3,222.01	£3,068.58	7.00	£30.00	£660.00	£871.43	£4,630.01	10.56	
4	30/11/2007	N	50695	£3,679.40	£3,504.19	6.91	£30.00	£660.00	£871.43	£5,065.62	9.99	
5	31/12/2007	N	57138	£4,706.39	£4,482.28	7.84	£30.00	£660.00	£871.43	£6,043.70	10.58	
6	31/01/2008	N	39562	£3,325.42	£3,167.08	8.01	£30.00	£660.00	£871.43	£4,728.50	11.95	
7	29/02/2008	N	30130	£2,583.64	£2,460.80	8.17	£30.00	£660.00	£871.43	£4,022.23	13.35	12.63 +
8	31/03/2008	N	60698	£4,936.19	£4,720.18	7.78	£30.00	£660.00	£871.43	£6,281.61	10.35	VAT = 13.20
9	30/04/2008	N	48823	£4,046.03	£3,853.36	7.89	£30.00	£660.00	£871.43	£5,414.79	11.09	
10	31/05/2008	N	34244	£2,959.85	£2,818.90	8.23	£30.00	£660.00	£871.43	£4,380.33	12.79	
11	30/06/2008	N	29689	£2,636.19	£2,510.66	8.40	£30.00	£660.00	£871.43	£4,072.09	13.62	
12	31/07/2008	N	27506	£2,453.87	£2,337.02	8.50	£30.00	£660.00	£871.43	£3,898.45	14.17	
13	31/08/2008	N	37262	£3,977.10	£3,787.71	11.74	£30.00	£660.00	£871.43	£5,349.14	15.58	
14	30/09/2008	N	32610	£4,312.27	£4,106.92	12.59	£30.00	£660.00	£871.43	£5,668.35	17.38	
						8.43			Average price including uplift		12.631	12.53

£360.00   £36.00   £0.00

1	31/10/2008	N	48152	£5,951.71	£5,668.30	11.77	£30.00	£660.00	£0.00	£6,358.30	13.20	
2	30/11/2008	N	47610	£5,861.27	£5,582.16	11.72	£30.00	£660.00	£0.00	£6,272.16	13.17	
3	31/12/2008	N	54474	£6,843.04	£6,326.70	11.61	£30.00	£660.00	£0.00	£7,016.70	12.88	
4	31/01/2009	N	41584	£5,147.04	£4,901.84	11.79	£30.00	£660.00	£0.00	£5,591.84	13.45	
5	28/02/2009	N	30142	£3,831.52	£3,649.07	12.11	£30.00	£660.00	£0.00	£4,339.07	14.40	
6	31/03/2009	N	40931	£5,087.34	£4,845.09	11.84	£30.00	£660.00	£0.00	£5,535.09	13.52	13.39 + VAT = 14.06
7	30/04/2009	N	39698	£4,921.83	£4,687.27	11.81	£30.00	£660.00	£0.00	£5,377.27	13.55	
8	31/05/2009	N	33725	£4,268.95	£4,065.67	12.06	£30.00	£660.00	£0.00	£4,755.67	14.10	
9	30/06/2009	N	22772	£3,004.08	£2,861.03	12.56	£30.00	£660.00	£0.00	£3,551.03	15.59	
10	31/07/2009	N	22541	£2,990.23	£2,847.84	12.63	£30.00	£660.00	£0.00	£3,537.84	15.70	
11	31/08/2009	N	27515	£3,577.74	£3,407.37	12.38	£30.00	£660.00	£0.00	£4,097.37	14.89	
						12.03			Average price including uplift		14.04	14.06

135

Referring back to Mr. Royle's letter of the 4th October 2010 (reference two) he states: "for the year 2006-2007 there has been a substantial undercharge to unit owners". The charge was in fact exactly in line with the contract price of 7.06p per unit. He further states "and for 2008-2009 the rate charged should have been 14.11p and not 14.06p per unit". Now kindly refer to the factual analysis. It all becomes very confusing doesn't it? But for the seriousness of it all it could well be described as a fraudulent farce.

Regarding his comments "we pay the electric bills monthly but only recover these from our customers yearly in arrear", this gives thought to the fact that he is not happy with this re-payment method by the Fell End customers. I'm sure he was quite content with me and everybody else having to pay our annual site fees one year in advance plus the current annual deposit of £800.00 one and a half years in advance.

On the 14th February 2011 Mr. Royle wrote to my solicitor, part of which is as follows: "Our financial controller has advised me that the total amount spent by us on electrical repairs and renewals at Fell End Caravan Park for the financial year 2006-2007 was £10,000 and for 2007-2008 the figure was £70,000… and involved the renewal of all the cabling". This work was in fact carried out during the year 2010 (two thousand and ten). I know, I was there.

20. FROM DESPAIR TO DELIVERANCE

I wrote earlier on in Part I about the divine intervention of fate. In this connection I will now enlighten you as to what took place.

What I needed for the 'Cooper Crusade' to continue was a top-class solicitor. You know, the £250.00 + per hour merchants. Without this high level of support I knew my intended and renewed campaign was doomed from the outset. End of story – goodnight – to wonder for ever.

I contemplated risking part of my liquid assets but in the event of losing, or indeed making a draw, in the ensuing legal battle would be too much to bear. I trust you will agree I had already lost far more than enough in other ways. We often read about the amount of awarded costs, often appearing, to me anyway, hugely excessive. Also frightening when you consider defeat. A defeat which would exacerbate our financial losses to date. There was also the potential lessening of morale together with the financial self-supporting element to consider. I thought as usual, the rogues, the fraudsters, the conspirators would get off scot-free. I became generally dispirited with life.

My selfishness and somewhat egotistical nature blinded me to the fact that my wife, since her Greek sabbatical had been quietly (as is her nature) re-creating a fresh dimension to our new home and lifestyle. Her amazing support together with that of my family gave me renewed vigour for life's future challenges (we all know that from time to time these have to be faced, don't we?).

THEN CAME THE TURNING POINT. Out of the blue and over a pint my son said to me "why don't you have a word with John Lord?".

In years gone by John Lord played rugby for Windermere R.U.F.C. Cumbria and at the same time as my son Jono. In many more years gone by I had the pleasure of playing alongside John's father, Bob Lord, for the same team. In fact Bob and I have represented Cumbria (then Cumberland and Westmorland). Forty plus years later Bob gave me his son's contact details. With some trepidation I telephoned John. He was not only too pleased to assist in my cause but pointed out his legal forte was in the investigation etc. of fraud. Including the charging of electricity! He was a partner in the internationally renowned firm of Irwin Mitchell. In my opening question to him regarding his costs he replied "let's see how we go on first". And so it was left until the outcome was in sight.

21. ROYLE'S RUINATION

In establishing the complete truth what better way than to transfer into my book, where appropriate, the actual dialogue that took place between Irwin Mitchell, my solicitors and represented by John Lord (J.L.) and the Pure Leisure Group represented by their group solicitor and company secretary who signs himself off as 'Chris Royle' (C.R.). On this note, I commence with the opening letter (salvo) dated the 10th February 2012 from J.L. to C.R. (reference A2). This particular communication will, I feel, determine to a large degree the 'heart and soul' of the matter. Just within this letter's fourteen day deadline for replying, an email was received dated the 27th February 2012 from C.R. (reference B2) A copy of J.L.'s follow-up letter dated 9th March 2012 (reference C2) to this email is shown herein. This was ignored by C.R.. On the 12th March 2012 he wrote to J.L. (reference D2) referring to J.L.'s letter of the 10th February as the 16th February 2012 (reference A2). J.L. replied on the 16th March 2012 (reference E2) copy shown herein. This letter was acknowledged by C.R. via email on the 16th April 2012 (reference F2). A period of correspondence approaching two months. I trust also you will have picked up the miserable, inadequate, brazen and bluff-filled contents of C.R.'s letter (reference D2) together with its six (typing?) errors (perhaps even the typist was becoming nervous?)

With reference to John Lord's use of the word 'estoppel' and not knowing its meaning I had to look it up. Confident in the belief there are one or two others of my book's faithful readership being in the same boat here is my dictionary's explanation: "A rule of evidence whereby a person is precluded from denying the truth of a statement of a fact he has previously asserted". So there we are. We live and learn!

Reference A2

Your Ref:
Our Ref: JJL/Cooper

10 February 2012

John Lord
john.lord@irwinmitchell.com
Direct Dial: 0161 838 7278

Dear Sirs

Our Client: Septimus Cooper and Others

We are instructed on behalf of the above named.

We have considered the correspondence passing between you and our client and we have also considered the correspondence passing between you and our client's former solicitors, Ratcliffe & Bibby of Lancaster. Please treat this letter as a letter of claim although in light of the correspondence already entered into between you and our client we would suggest that you require no more than 14 days in which to evaluate your position and provide us with your proposals for resolving this dispute.

Background

Our client previously sited his caravan at Fell End Caravan Park which is one of a number of caravan parks which are owned and controlled by you. The salient aspects of your terms and conditions provide;

3.2 Pitch fees are reviewed on an annual basis. The Company will give you three months notice in writing of any increase in Pitch fees, having regard to any changes in the cost of living, sums spent by the Company on the park & or its facilities, changes in the costs of salaries/wages paid to our staff, changes in the length of the Season or any other relevant factor.

3.7 Electricity charges will be payable within 14 days of demand. Charges will be based on the guidelines of OFGEM.

Our client engaged in correspondence with Energy Cost Management (ECM) and they wrote to our client on 16 April 2009 and stated;

"I hope this helps to clarify why you have seen such an increase in your costs and I can assure you that Pure Leisure and ECM go to great lengths to ensure you get the best deal possible at every Contract renewal".

On 14 February 2011 your Mr Royle, Group Solicitor and Company Secretary, wrote to our client's former solicitors (following a significant period of delay) and stated inter alia;

"Our financial controller has advised me that the total amount spent by us on electrical repairs and renewals at Fell End Caravan Park for the financial year 2006-07 was £10,000 and for 2007-08 the figure was £70,000. This latter figure included the substantial cost of completely upgrading the whole electrical system at the Park and involved the renewal of all the cabling. It was decided that the fairest way of dealing with the recovery of this amount was to relate only part of the same to the electrical charges which meant that those customers who consumed more electricity would effectively be paying their fair share of the costs of this upgrade. Otherwise to have included the whole of the same in a pitch fee increase would impact unfavourably on those of our customers who used their caravans only infrequently and so consumed less electricity".

And further:

"....the reason for this is that we possess considerable purchasing power because of the number of Parks that we own and this reflects in low competitive purchase prices we have obtained the benefit of which has been passed on to our customers."

Without prejudice to what appears below with respect to the assertion of agency made by ECM, we anticipate that you are aware of the restrictions imposed by OFGEM on resellers of electricity who may not generate a profit on the electricity which they go on to supply to end users. You are accordingly not permitted to generate any profit whatsoever on the resale of electricity (if indeed you are a reseller which is a matter for debate).

The Contractual Position

<u>Your Terms and Conditions</u>

We note that you believe that you are able to unilaterally decide to increase the electricity charges in order to artificially ensure that there is no increase in the pitch fees. We do not consider that you are able to operate in this way because the electricity charges referred to within your terms and conditions are clearly intended to relate solely to the cost of the electricity supplied rather than the absorbed costs of improvements which are made in order to improve the electrical network within the Park. Clause 3.2 specifically allows you to increase the pitch fees in a wide range of circumstances which undoubtedly includes the stated need to spend £70,000 improving the electrical system. Such works represent maintenance and improvement works and the cost of such items should, in accordance with your own terms and conditions, be wholly absorbed into the cost of the pitch fees because the term "electricity charges" relates solely to the cost of the electricity supplied.

We consider that you have therefore breached your obligations to our client by operating in the manner set out within your letter dated 14 February 2011. This is because you have increased the cost of your electricity charges in order to artificially maintain lower pitch charges (no doubt as a result of the likely negative connotations for prospective users of the park should the pitch fees increase).

Your terms and conditions also stipulate that "Charges will be based on the guidelines of OFGEM". OFGEM do not make provision for Park operators to increase the cost of electricity in order to artificially maintain lower pitch fees. OFGEM are concerned with the price of electricity and ensuring that resellers do not artificially inflate the price of electricity or indeed sell electricity at a price which is in excess of the sums which they have paid when acquiring the electricity. Therefore, the unit price paid by you when you purchased electricity from E.On must be exactly the same as the unit price charged to our client and other park users. You have already candidly admitted that you have inflated the price of electricity in order to

141

purchased electricity from E.On must be exactly the same as the unit price charged to our client and other park users. You have already candidly admitted that you have inflated the price of electricity in order to artificially maintain lower pitch fees. This conduct represents a clear breach of contract and a failure to comply with OFGEM guidelines.

Your obligations as our client's agent/your obligations as a reseller

ECM have represented that you and they "go to great lengths" to ensure that our client and other Park users get the best possible deal at every Contract renewal. This suggests that you and ECM are acting as agents for the benefit of their principals (being our client and other park users). It is trite law that an agent owes a number of fiduciary obligations to its principal. Bowstead and Reynolds on Agency succinctly set out such duties at Art 43 6-038 and Art 45 6-055 as;

- To act in good faith
- Not make a profit out of his trust (secret profit)
- Not act for his own benefit or the benefit of a third person without the informed consent of his principal
- The duty to make full disclosure

We consider that the admissions contained within your letter dated 14 February 2011 evidence that you have breached all of the above principles of agency. By unlawfully increasing the cost of electricity charges in order to artificially maintain lower pitch fees you have failed to act in good faith. By increasing prices above the actual unit charge paid to E.On you have made a profit out of your trust and you have made a secret profit. You have also self evidently acted for your own benefit in a manner which is highly prejudicial to our client and others and you have failed to make full disclosure to our client (although he has admittedly received fuller disclosure than others) or the other park users who have been prejudiced by your actions.

In circumstances where a secret profit has been made by an agent (and it is clear that you have been charging our client and other park users a higher price for each unit of electricity than you are legally entitled to), you have a positive obligation to account to our client (and the other park users) for the profits generated.

The position is broadly the same if a Court decides that you are not an agent but that you are in fact a reseller. Your own terms and conditions preclude your ability to behave in the way in which you have and you have self evidently not complied with OFGEM's guidelines. In such circumstances, you must account to our client and other park users for the difference between the amount charged by you to our client and other park users and the price paid by you for the electricity purchased from E.On.

This obligation arises with respect to all of your parks and affects all users who have a right to receive payment either under the principles of agency or as a consequence of profiteering from your position as a reseller. Those liabilities are recoverable subject to the Limitation Act 1980 although a Court may be convinced that a 6 year limitation period should not apply in these circumstances as your conduct would appear to be both deliberate and calculated.

We should be grateful to receive a copy of your supply licence with OFGEM entitling you to operate as a reseller in order to enable us to consider whether a Court is more likely to identify you as an agent or a reseller. If you do not in fact have a licence then we would ask you to clarify how you view yourself and how it is that you believe you can adhere to OFGEM's guidelines when you are not in fact licensed by them.

The Calculation of VAT

We have observed that you have charged VAT on the inflated invoices which have been rendered. VAT is rendered at 5% which confirms to us that you accept that the electricity supplied is for domestic or non business use and this will be the basis upon which you acquire electricity from E.On. However, we are concerned by the contents of your letter dated 14 February 2011 because any work undertaken with respect to improving the site should result in a VAT liability calculated at the rate of either 17.5% or 20%. Pitch fees attract VAT at 20% so by operating in a contrived manner whereby the genuine costs of the works identified are absorbed into the electricity charges, the true extent of your VAT liabilities have not been properly revealed to HMRC. Indeed, VAT at 5% ought not to have been charged because the actual services provided went far beyond the mere provision of electricity and ought to have attracted VAT either at 17.5% or 20%.

We should be obliged if you would provide us with your observations with respect to this issue as we have serious concerns with respect to the manner in which you have charged VAT because it would appear to be designed to reduce the tax which is lawfully payable and therefore you may have committed a fraud on HMRC.

We should of course make it clear that estoppel is likely to prevent you from seeking to re-engineer the VAT position and attempting to recover additional sums from our client and other park users. We do not however think that estoppel is likely to prevent HMRC collecting any sums which may be due to it as a consequence of your efforts to artificially maintain lower pitch fees by absorbing the costs associated with maintenance and improvements into the electricity charges and then applying VAT at 5%.

Remedy

Whilst we are surprised by the contents of your Mr Royle's letter dated 14 February 2011 (which appears to us to have been written to deal with the exigencies of the moment), we are also surprised that you have failed to resolve matters despite numerous opportunities which have been presented to you over a number of years, our client is prepared to give you a further 14 days in which to consider your position and advance proposals either on an open or without prejudice basis.

Our right to secure instructions from other parties affected by your conduct together with all of our client's rights remain expressly reserved.

We look forward to hearing from you within the prescribed period.

Yours faithfully

IRWIN MITCHELL LLP

Reference B2

Page 1 of 2

B 2.

Sara White

From: John Lord
Sent: 27 February 2012 15:58
To: Sara White
Subject: FW: Your client Septimus Cooper

send copy of this to SP

John Lord
Partner
Commercial Litigation Team
IM Business
For and on behalf of Irwin Mitchell
Bauhaus
Rossetti Place
27 Quay Street
Manchester
M3 4 AW

Tel: 0870 1500 100
Direct Dial: 0161 838 7276
Direct Fax: 0870 197 3552
Mobile: 07760 775 330
Email: john.lord@irwinmitchell.com
www.irwinmitchell.com

From: Chris Royle [mailto:Chris.Royle@pureleisuregroup.com]
Sent: 27 February 2012 15:43
To: John Lord
Subject: Your client Septimus Cooper

Dear Sirs

Receipt is acknowledged of your letter to us dated 16th February last.

We are considering all that you say and will respond to you fully in the matter within the next fourteen days.

Yours faithfully

Chris Royle
Group Solicitor & Company Secretary
t: +44 (0) 1524 784227
e: chris.royle@pureleisuregroup.com

PURE LEISURE GROUP
South Lakeland House, Yealand Redmayne, Carnforth, Lancs. LA5 9RN
w: www.pureleisuregroup.com

Billing Aquadrome   South Lakeland Leisure Village   Fell End & Hall More Caravan Parks   Tydd St Giles Golf & Leisure Estate

27/02/2012

Reference C2

Your Ref:
Our Ref: JJL/Cooper

Pure Leisure Group
South Lakeland House
Yealand Redmayne
Carnforth
Lancashire
LS5 9RN
VIA FAX (0)1524 782243 **AND POST**

09 March 2012

John Lord
john.lord@irwinmitchell.com
Direct Dial: 0161 838 7278

Dear Sirs

Our Client: Septimus Cooper and Others

Thank you for your email dated 27 February 2012.

Our client is naturally disappointed by your failure to respond to our correspondence within the 14 days prescribed. This is all the more surprising in light of the fact that this dispute has been extensively ventilated in correspondence over a number of years.

We enclose herewith a copy of a letter received from Mr William Moore dated 6 March 2012. The contents of this letter suggests that there may be other anomalies with respect to the payment of VAT and whilst we do not act for Mr Moore at this stage it would be helpful if you would confirm whether VAT was applied to demands for rates as alleged. If such demands were made, what happened to the sums raised by the erroneous VAT demands? Were they repaid to the Licensees, paid to HMRC (and held on trust by them for the benefit of the Licensees) or retained by the company and accounted for in the company's books and records?

Our own client has suggested that he was the subject of other VAT overcharges beyond those already highlighted by us within our correspondence.

We look forward to you commenting upon the allegation that you habitually charged VAT either at the incorrect rate or without lawful justification.

Your response is due by 12 March 2012.

Yours faithfully

IRWIN MITCHELL LLP

Encl

6.3.12 Mr William Moore
20 Aynam Road
Kendal
Cumbria
LA9 7DW
Formerly of 69 Fell End Caravan Site

To Whom it may Concern

When I recieved my first rent and rates bill from Pure Leisure I was being charged VAT on top of my rates.

I spoke to Tim Farron about the fact I was being charged VAT and he informed me that VAT is not payable on rates, I informed the office at Fell End what Mr. Farron. had said and they refunded me the VAT. I don't know how many other people were charged VAT but on reflection of the way the side was run. excesive rent, Electric, and gas prices I would not be suprised if this was not common practice

Yours Faithfully
W Moore.

AUTHOR'S NOTE

THE TIM FARRON REFERRED TO IS THE LOCAL M.P. AND PRESIDENT OF THE LIBERAL DEMOCRATS.

Reference D2

D2

pure leisure
GROUP
UK & INTERNATIONAL HOLIDAY HOMES

Messrs. Irwin Mitchell llp
Solicitors
Bauhas Rossetti Place
27 Quay Street
Manchester M3 4AR

WITHOUT PREJUDICE

Ref JJL/Cooper

12th March 2012

Dear Sirs

Your client Septimus Cooper

We have now had an opportunity of considering your letter to us of 16th February.

We think that no useful purposed will be served in commenting upon the points that you make in your letter save to say that we disagree with all of them. There is no question that ECM were agents for your clients and we do even propose to comment on your allegations with regard to VAT save that we find it offensive that you should put in writing that we are committing a fraud on the Revenue.

We have however reconsidered our position in regard to the settlement of your client's claim and we have decided that entirely without prejudice and without accepting any liability we are prepared to reinstate the offer of £1000 as an ex gratia payment to your client without admission of liability and in full and final settlement of all claims that your client has against us. We would also expect your client to sign a confidentiality undertaking.

Upon hearing from you that this is agreed we will send you our cheque for £1000 and a receipt and confidentiality undertaking to be signed by your client. In whose favour should the cheque be drawn?

Yours faithfully

Chris Royle
Group Solicitor and Company Secretary

PURE LEISURE GROUP

South Lakeland House
Yealand Redmayne, Carnforth
Lancashire. LA5 9RN. UK.

t: +44 (0) 1524 781918
f: +44 (0) 1524 782243
e: enquiries@pureleisuregroup.cc
i: www.pureleisuregroup.com

Reference E2

Your Ref:
Our Ref: JJL/Cooper

Pure Leisure Group
South Lakeland House
Yealand Redmayne
Carnforth
Lancashire
LS5 9RN

VIA FAX (0)1524 782243 **AND POST**

27 March 2012

John Lord
john.lord@irwinmitchell.com
Direct Dial: 0161 838 7278

Dear Sirs

Our Client: Septimus Cooper and Others

Thank you for your letter dated 12 March 2012 which was received by us on 16 March 2012

The Civil Procedure Rules ("the CPR") govern the way in which, in this Country, parties conduct themselves. You are bound by the CPR in exactly the same way as any other party who is engaged in litigation. The letter which we wrote to you was a letter of claim and you have a positive obligation to fully respond to it. Put bluntly, it is not good enough for you to state "we think that no useful purposed (sic) will be served in commenting upon the points that you make in your letter save to say that we disagree with all of them."

Our client has made a number of serious allegations against you with respect to your treatment of VAT and the way in which he and other site users have been exposed to VAT liabilities. Further, our client has asked you for a detailed explanation with respect to whether you view yourself as a reseller or whether you and ECM view yourselves as agents. Whilst you have suggested that there is "no question that ECM were agents..." their letter dated 16 April 2009 clearly seeks to suggest that they and you engage with electricity suppliers of the site users. This clearly suggests a relationship of agency.

Whilst your letter says "we do even propose to comment on your allegations with regard to VAT" you do not actually comment on the allegations beyond suggesting that you take offence at our suggestion that you may have committed a fraud on HMRC. However, our suggestion that you may have committed a fraud on HMRC arises as a consequence of your own correspondence dated 14 February 2011 and your reluctance to provide a full explanation with respect to your treatment of VAT does little to change our views.

Our client wishes to evaluate the strength of his claim by reference to a response from you which complies with your obligations pursuant to the CPR. We invite you to provide a full response to the letter of claim failing which our client will issue proceedings and obtain full financial disclosure of your books and records and we will fully interrogate the VAT position. If following our interrogation of the position we believe that your client has committed a fraud against our client and others, we will thereafter amend our client's claim and bring the issue of fraud before the Court.

We note your derisory offer of £1,000 and we confirm that the offer is rejected not least because it is even worse than the offer made by you previously. Therefore, it is not a reinstatement of your previous offer at all.

We consider that our client (and other park users) are entitled to substantial damages from you. We consider that there are multiple claimants who are able to advance claims against you as a result of over charging at the Carnforth site and we would not be at all surprised to discover similar practices at other parks which you operate. We also consider that there is a direct causative link between your conduct and our client's decision to sell his caravan to you at a price which did not reflect its true value. We reserve our client's right to advance claims against you in relation to this transaction.

Our client has asked us to ascertain whether Mr Morphet is aware of the issues relevant to this dispute and whether he is aware of the admissions contained within Mr Royle's letter dated 14 February 2011. Please clarify whether Mr Morphet is aware of matters and please also confirm whether you revealed to KPMG the dubious accounting practices which are described within Mr Royle's letter dated 14 February 2011 as these practices raise serious concerns with respect to the auditing of the company's accounts.

Unless you adopt a serious approach to this litigation and advance realistic proposals for settlement within the next 7 days our client (and others we suspect) will advance claims against you.

We look forward to hearing from you within the prescribed period.

Yours faithfully

IRWIN MITCHELL LLP

Reference F2

Direct Dial: 0161 838 7276

Direct Fax: 0870 197 3552

Mobile: 07760 775 330

Email: john.lord@irwinmitchell.com

www.irwinmitchell.com

From: Chris Royle [mailto:Chris.Royle@pureleisuregroup.com]
Sent: 16 April 2012 10:45
To: John Lord
Subject: Septimus Cooper and others

Dear Sir

We acknowledge receipt of your letter dated 27th March.

We have instructed outside solicitors to act for us in this matter. They are Weightmans LLP of India Buildings Water Street Liverpool L2 0GS. The person who is dealing with the matter there is Tom Collins email Tom.Collins@Weightmans.com Please address all future correspondence to them direct.

Weightmans ask that you give them a further fourteen days in which to respond to your correspondence as they have only just recently been instructed. They will be providing a full response to your clients allegations

Yours faithfully

Chris Royle

Group Solicitor & Company Secretary

t: +44 (0) 1524 784227

e: chris.royle@pureleisuregroup.com

I have commented quite sparsely so far regarding the contents of the correspondence passing between Irwin Mitchell (I.M.) and the Pure Leisure Group (P.L.G.) i.e. the letters A2 to F2. There is not a lot to add as most of it I believe is self-explanatory. I'm confident you are coming to your own conclusions, whatever they may be. Absorbing without difficulty the story as it unfolds. Getting my "two pennorth" in however will hopefully give you an inside perspective on matters. It may also be an irritation on your thoughts!

Mr. Royle's proud spreadsheet presentation, letter reference one, would I feel in his mind bring down the curtain on the whole shooting match. If he's been having sleepless nights they would now be over. That would be, however, until the arrival on his desk of my solicitors letter (reference A2). Even so Mr. Royle found that this letter was only deserving of an email (reference B2) and which indeed took six days to send an acknowledgement only. My solicitors (I.M.) letter (reference C2) adds salt to the wound. A reply from Mr. Royle (reference D2) you will have noticed was then received on the deadline. This letter I have previously commented on. I would suggest that John Lord in his letter (reference E2) now had P.L.G.'s group solicitor and company secretary in a vice-like grip and in classic terrier-type fashion was not going to let go. Mr. Royle I felt was done for, hence his calling-in of outside solicitors i.e. his email (reference F2).

With reference to Mr. Royle's final communication (reference F2) one cannot help but detect a sense of beleaguerment and utter deflation in his writings. I knew then, he knew then and my legal man John Lord knew then, his game was up. A battle however still had to be fought, and won, against one of the top legal firms in the land. Meanwhile, back at his web, Mr. Royle had become entangled in a wretched situation. One which there was no escape from. His only and forlorn hope now lay with outside solicitors. It had evidently all become too much for him. His only slight consolation was that he lived many miles away from his place of employ. This was in Moore, Warrington. Out of the firing line, so to speak.

Upon reflection however do you think he actually had any feelings of guilt? No regret, no conscience, shameless indeed. Over the years how many other deceits of this nature had he been responsible for? We are all aware that when a solicitor seriously contravenes the boundaries of impeccability in respect of the law's code of conduct he/she is "struck off" with the expectancy of worse to come.

Mr. Royle's last letter did however signal the end of Fell End Park's management game. It would not be wrong to call it "pass the time-bomb" e.g. Marianne Gaskell (E.C.M) – Alan Green – John Morphet – Trevor White – Alan Green – Christopher Royle – Tony Fox -Weightmans.

As you know, Weightmans solicitors of Liverpool were instructed by the Pure Leisure Group to act for them on the 16th April 2012. Nine days later a Mr. Tony Fox, the managing director of P.L.G. telephoned me with a view to "reaching a compromise Septimus". Indeed, he wanted to reach a settlement there and then. We met at my home two days later. He was, of course, aware of Weightmans recent involvement. So, why this meeting? Perhaps a little collusion had taken place to bring the matter to an immediate closure. Pats on the back all round.

Several untruths emanated from Mr. Fox's mouth whenever the honest answer would incriminate his company, e.g. "each of our parks has a different electric supplier". When cornered he counter-attacked e.g. – "suggesting I was a blackmailer – their V.A.T. position was 'perfect' – John would defend any action for another three years if necessary – if John had been at this meeting I would have got what for."

A lot more dialogue took place including "hush" monies of £4,000.00 (four thousand pounds) being offered. He also continued addressing me incessantly as Septimus. The traditional offering of tea did not take place and, yes, he shook my hand on departing.

Although perhaps irrelevant to my cause Mr. Fox's past business track record of failure is up there with the worst. He left P.L.G. (John's company) in April 2013.

22. THE SOLICITORS. THEIR WRITINGS AND THE OUTCOME

The above is now shown herein which gives an opportunity for us ordinary folk to see how the top-level legal fraternity inter-communicate (vie) with each other. Normally, if and when we are to use their services only your own legal team's correspondence to you is seen. It also provides me with an opening to show you, in the interests of fairness, the Pure Leisure Group solicitor's side of the story. I hope, indeed I am confident, you will find it both informative and interesting. Where I believe it is necessary my comments intervene between the correspondence. I do realise this will interrupt the "legal flow/interchanges" but trust you will agree these intrusions attempt keep matters in perspective.

Weightmans, Pure Leisure Group's (P.L.G.) solicitors at last entered the fray, following my solicitors letter to P.L.G. of the 6th August 2012. You will recall earlier on in the book Mr. Royle in his email to Mr. Lord (reference F) and dated the 16th April 2012 stating: "We have instructed outside solicitors to act for us in this matter. They are Weightmans LLP...". A delay of approximately four months.

With reference to their opening letter of the 15th August 2012 they refer to a proposed press release, a copy of which is enclosed herein. It is shown for your interest. Every word, in essence is true although its progress, not quite reaching the intended end, can be followed as you read on.

irwinmitchell

Media Information

xx.08.12

CUMBRIAN MAN SEEKS TO CLAIM HOLIDAY HOME FUEL OVERCHARGE

- Frustrated Victim Believes Hundreds of Other Holiday Park Users Could Be Affected

A [aged] year old man who claims he and other park users have paid thousands of pounds more than they should for using electricity whilst staying on a Lake District holiday park, has instructed specialist lawyers and says he fears the overcharging may relate to other parks across the country.

Septimus Cooper, from Milnthorpe near Kendal, believes the Lancashire-based holiday company, Pure Leisure Group Ltd (Pure), overcharged him hundreds of pounds between 2008 and 2011 whilst he stayed at Fell End Caravan Park, which is owned by Pure.

The holiday company, which has seven other parks across the UK, have subsequently argued in correspondence with Mr Cooper that they purposefully 'marked up' the cost of the electricity used during the period to cover the costs of upgrading the park's electric wiring system, which included the renewal of all cabling. Mr Cooper argues however that the company had not informed him of their plans and claims they were not legally entitled to generate a margin on the electricity supplied.

Expert lawyers at leading national law firm, Irwin Mitchell, acting for Mr Cooper argue Pure breached its own terms and conditions along with OFGEM guidelines, as they sold the electricity at a different unit price to the price they paid for it.

Arguing on behalf of Mr Cooper, Irwin Mitchell claims the company, without openly informing holiday park tenants, resold electricity purchased from its supplier to park users at a higher unit price – something which is expressly forbidden and in breach of OFGEM guidelines.

Please Note: Page 1 of 3

Media Information

irwinmitchell

John Lord, a Partner at the firm's Manchester office who specialises in dealing with commercial disputes within the energy sector, said: "It appears that the Pure Leisure Group increased the price of electricity units that it charged to residents on the park in order to pay for work at the park.

"OFGEM do not make provision for any holiday park business to inflate the cost of electricity whether to pay for improvements work or for any other reason. The unit price paid by users of the site should be the same as that which Pure paid when it purchased electricity from its own supplier. We intend to argue before Court that there is no scope for Pure to generate a margin when re-selling the electricity to its own customers."

Mr Cooper, who purchased his Fell End holiday home in [20xx] but sold it last year following the dispute, explained: "I believe that Pure have illegally overcharged me for the cost of using electricity at the park. There are hundreds of others who have lived on the park during the same period and I'm concerned that others could be out of pocket as a result."

In addition to allegedly 'marking up' the cost of electricity, Mr Cooper asserts that the company may have failed to pay the correct levels of VAT.

Mr Cooper commented: "Pure appears to have charged 5% VAT. If as according to them, however, the higher electricity unit price was used to pay for the cost of improving the campsite's electrical infrastructure, it ought to have attracted a higher rate of VAT when passed on to customers."

Pure Leisure Group is based in Carnforth and has a turnover of £36m. It operates eight UK-based holiday parks, two golf leisure parks and Westmoreland Park in Barbados. Fell End Caravan Park consists mainly of privately owned caravans, rental caravans and camping pods. The complex includes a restaurant, an indoor leisure pool and an air conditioned gym.

John Lord added: "It is our client's understanding that others on the Fell End park will have paid similar amounts and that they too could be entitled to a significant amount of money back.

Please Note: Page 2 of 3

irwinmitchell

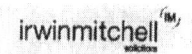

Media Information

"We would certainly urge anyone who has stayed at this or any of the other seven Pure Leisure parks to investigate what they have been charged. Should they feel they have paid more than they should, they should contact us as it is our intention to issue Court proceedings against Pure."

Ends

Contact Details:

David Shirt
PR Manager
Irwin Mitchell
Tel: 0161 838 3094
Mob: 07720 509912
david.shirt@irwinmitchell.com

Irwin Mitchell

In April 2011, Irwin Mitchell was the first major law firm to announce that it would become an Alternative Business Structure and that it would seek external investment with the implementation of the final stage of the Legal Services Act. It was also one of the first firms to begin the application process when the Solicitors Regulation Authority began accepting applications on January 3rd.

One of the largest law firms in the UK, Irwin Mitchell was first established in 1912 and is celebrating its centenary this year. The firm employs more than 2100 staff and has more than 150 Partners helping over 200,000 clients a year. There are offices in Birmingham, Glasgow, Leeds, London, Manchester, Newcastle, Bristol and Sheffield as well as a consulting office in Leicester and two offices in Spain. For more information visit www.irwinmitchell.com.

The firm won an award for its innovative corporate strategy and was also named in the Industry Pioneers category at the annual 'FT Innovative Lawyers' awards in 2011. It was ranked in the Top 50 litigators in the world by The Lawyer magazine and in 2011 was named as one of the leading companies in the country for commitment to local communities in the prestigious Business in the Community's (BITC) annual Corporate Responsibility Index.

Other accolades include being listed among the top five Most Diverse Law firms in the UK by the Black Solicitors Network. The Legal Sector Alliance also found Irwin Mitchell to have the 2nd Lowest Carbon Footprint of any UK law firm.

Please Note: Page 3 of 3

Your Ref:
Our Ref: JJL/CS/BLS-COMLIT/1295266-1

Pure Leisure Group
South Lakeland House
Yealand Redmayne
Carnforth
Lancashire
LA5 9RN

06 August 2012

John Lord
john.lord@irwinmitchell.com
Tel: 0161 838 7276

WITHOUT PREJUDICE

Dear Sirs

Our Client: Septimus Cooper

We have put your offer to our client.

Our client has requested that you immediately make payment of the sums which are due to him with respect to the overcharging. Our client's best estimate with respect to the overcharging is £700 pa x 4 years equating to £2,800. There is no reason why this sum should not be paid by return.

It is our client's intention to notify other customers of Pure Leisure Ltd, HMRC, the SFO, OFGEM and the press so as to ensure that your conduct can be properly scrutinised by the public and by the authorities.

Our client has reflected on his position and decided that your conduct is so serious that his civic duties dictate that he must highlight your conduct so that you are compelled to reimburse those who have been prejudiced by your unlawful conduct and also answer to those who may wish to investigate your activities.

Yours faithfully

IRWIN MITCHELL LLP

Weightmans

Liverpool L3 9QJ
DX 718100 Liverpool 16
www.weightmans.com

Irwin Mitchell
DX 14368
Manchester 1

By DX and fax: 0161 839 9804

Contact: Tom Collins

T: 0151 242 6939
E: tom.collins@weightmans.com

Our ref: MGR TCO LHE 445876 4
Your ref: JJL/CS/Septimus Cooper/1351943-1

15 August 2012

Dear Sirs

Re: Dispute with Septimus Cooper

We act for Mr John Morphet, trading as Pure Leisure, the owner of Fell End Caravan Park.

We have been passed a copy of your letter to our client dated 8 August 2012.

We understand that you are instructed by Mr Septimus Cooper only. To that end we shall address the issues raised by you on behalf of Mr Cooper only.

In your letter you seek confirmation of the steps taken by our client to contact E.ON, OFGEM and HMRC and also steps taken to notify all of Pure Leisure's customers of overcharging.

Our client has confirmed already and confirms again that he is in the process of providing refunds to all customers who may have been overcharged. This includes your client and we understand that the refund will be made shortly. The obligation on our client is to use reasonable endeavours to provide the refund and he is so doing.

To that end your client's complaint will have been satisfied. We do not therefore see the need to address you further on your queries. You appear to suggest, and indeed your press release appears to suggest, that you are looking to put together a group action. Again, we understand you are only instructed by Mr Cooper and as we say above he is now to receive a refund. As you are not instructed by other parties we will not address the point further. What is clear however is that as refunds are to be made there is no requirement for any court action.

So far as the press release is concerned it is not a 'balanced' press release as you suggest. In any event in light of this letter there is no requirement to send the release.

Notwithstanding we make clear that the overcharging was an innocent error and accordingly the suggestion of 'purposefully 'mark[ing] up' the cost of electricity' leads to the innuendo that our client

Page 2

Our ref: MGR TCO LHE 445876 4

Your ref: JJL/CS/Septimus Cooper/1351943-1

did so in order to take advantage of customers. This is wholly incorrect and is allegedly defamatory of our client. We expect you to confirm by return, and by no later than 4pm on 17 August 2012 that this comment will not be published. In the event that you do not provide such confirmation our client reserves all rights accordingly.

We look forward to hearing from you by return.

Yours faithfully

Weightmans LLP

On Monday 2 July, our Liverpool office moved to 100 Old Hall Street, Liverpool, L3 9QJ. Main telephone 0845 073 9900. Main fax 0845 073 9950. DX 718100 Liverpool 16

Your Ref: MGR TCO LHE 445876 4
Our Ref: JJL/CS/Sep Cooper/1381461-1

Weightmans LLP
Solicitors
DX 718100
LIVERPOOL 16

ALSO BY FAX: 0845 073 9950

16 August 2012

John Lord
john.lord@irwinmitchell.com
Tel: 0161 838 7276

Dear Sirs

Our Client: Septimus Cooper

Thank you for your letter dated 15 August 2012.

We are a little confused by your reference to you acting for Mr Morphet rather than the Pure Leisure Group. The VAT number appearing on the invoices received by our client is 514 3195 67. That is the VAT number of Mr Morphett.

The licence conditions identify the contracting parties as our client and "the Company" being Pure Leisure whose registered office is "South Lakeland House, A6, Yealand Redmayne, Carnforth, Lancs LA5 9RN". All correspondence between our client and Pure Leisure Group quotes a company number of 05113719 and the registered office of that company (being the Pure Leisure Group Ltd) is as above. Self evidently as an individual or sole trader Mr Morphett will not have a registered office.

It is clear that our client contracted with the Pure Leisure Group Ltd rather than Mr Morphett who is not identified within any of the contractual documentation entered into. Indeed, the Pure Leisure Group's officers wrote to our client and did not once suggest that the contracting party was in fact Mr Morphet.

If what you say is nevertheless correct our client and other park users have made substantial payments to Mr Morphett which were never due to Mr Morphett and our client and others have paid VAT on services provided by the Pure Leisure Group Ltd rather than Mr Morphett. Further, the disconnection of services to our client's caravan which would appear to have been undertaken by Mr Morphet rather than the contracting company must have been either unlawful or have been based on a misrepresentation of the rights enjoyed by the Pure Leisure Group Ltd.

Please provide a response to our assertion that our client contracted with Pure Leisure Group Ltd rather than Mr Morphet and all payments to Mr Morphet have been made under a mistake of fact and should be refunded to our client.

We now turn to the balance of your letter.

Our client has seen no evidence of your client's efforts to refund customers or otherwise notify them of the overcharging at the hands of the Pure Leisure Group Ltd. We take issue with your suggestion that the obligation is to "use reasonable endeavours" to locate the victims of overcharging. Your client has a positive obligation to use his best endeavours to refund monies which are not lawfully his and if he fails to adhere to these standards then he is likely to profit from his unlawful conduct. Please provide evidence of all your client is doing in order to discharge his responsibilities which by definition includes contacting OFGEM, HMRC and the electricity providers.

We notified the company of the issue of overcharging 6 months ago and yet even today not a single repayment has been made to any park user affected. Indeed, the proposal you make does not seem to take into account your client's obligation to pay interest which in our view should be paid in accordance with the principles underpinning the Late Payment Of Commercial Debts. Please confirm that interest will be paid on all refunds which are to be made.

We note your comments with respect to the draft press release. We note that your only objection to the press release is some vague argument with respect to defamation by innuendo. It cannot be in serious dispute that your client purposefully marked up the cost of electricity in order to pay for improvements to be made at the park. Without prejudice to other arguments set out in our earlier correspondence, your client ~~ms to be objecting to a statement of fact when it did indeed deliberately generate a margin on ~~tricity re-sold to the park users. The stated "purpose" was to improve the infrastructure at the park and is is made clear within the press release. The word "purposefully" seems to be the issue here and whilst we think your reference to defamation by innuendo fails to stand up to scrutiny we propose that this word is removed. We also feel that the release probably needs to be amended further in order to address the identity of the contracting party as more particularly identified above.

This is all the more so in light of your suggestion that the wording complained of is "allegedly defamatory of our client." Your client is not actually mentioned within the press release which means that you are bizarrely commenting upon an alleged defamation by innuendo which has nothing whatsoever to do with your client. This clearly puts your request for confirmation that the release will not be published into context but we would hope that the proposed amendments will ensure that this issue can be swiftly resolved so that the release is fair and balanced.

We look forward to hearing from you by the deadline imposed by you i.e. 4 pm on 17 August 2012.

Yours faithfully

IRWIN MITCHELL LLP

With regard to John Lord's (J.L.) comments in his letter to Weightmans (W) of the 16th August 2012 and in respect of the "reasonable endeavours" argument I would add the following: I have corresponded with thirty-two holiday home owners I came to know and who have left the park but were in residence at the time of the electric overcharging. Not one of them has contacted me saying a refund has been received. There must be many more, in respect of touring caravans with a seventy-seven pitch availability there must be hundreds who could have been contacted by the Pure Leisure Group, quite simply by using the security details demanded on their arrival at the park. Alternatively by P.L.G. advertising in their local newspaper etc.. My friend, who still has a tourer sited at the park 365 days a year tells me that subject to handing in his old used electric cards which cost him £7.50 per card he would receive a discount of £2.50 off the new cards, re-priced at £5.00. Based on the foregoing, I would suggest "reasonable endeavours" have not been implemented.

Weightmans

Weightmans LLP
100 Old Hall Street
Liverpool L3 9QJ

T +44(0)845 073 9900
F +44(0)845 073 9950
DX 716100 Liverpool 16
www.weightmans.com

Irwin Mitchell
DX 14368
Manchester 1

Contact: Tom Collins
T: 0151 242 6939
E: tom.collins@weightmans.com

Our ref: MGR TCO LHE 445876 4
Your ref: JJL/CS/Septimus Cooper/1351943-1

By DX and fax: 0161 839 9804

17 August 2012

Dear Sirs

Re: Dispute with Septimus Cooper

We refer to your letter dated 16 August 2012.

We reiterate that Fell End Caravan Park is owned by John Morphet trading as Pure Leisure.

The licence conditions are clear in that they refer to a contract between the holiday home owner/occupier and Pure Leisure (the trading name of Mr Morphet). There is no reference to Pure Leisure Group Limited as you suggest.

The fact that Pure Leisure is defined as "the Company" and it is said that it has a registered office does not mean that there is a contract with Pure Leisure Group Limited. There is simply no reference to Pure Leisure Group Limited. There is however reference to Pure Leisure. The invoices sent to your client are also in the name of Pure Leisure and bear Mr Morphet's VAT number as you note.

In the circumstances it is not correct that your client contracted with Pure Leisure Group Limited.

So far as the correspondence your client has received to date is concerned, that has not exclusively been on Pure Leisure Group Limited letterhead. In any event that does not change the fact that your client contracted with Mr Morphet. Furthermore, it is not correct that "not once" has it been suggested that the contracting party was Mr Morphet. In fact at a meeting between Tony Fox and your client Mr Fox explained he was a director of Pure Leisure Group Limited. He explained that Fell End was owned by John Morphet. He explained that he also had duties in relation to Pure Leisure. He made clear that he was representing Mr Morphet at that meeting. Your client will be able to confirm this to you.

In light of what we say above your assertion that payments have been made to Mr Morphet which were never due to Mr Morphet is wholly incorrect.

163

Page   2

Our ref: MGR TCO LHE 445876 4

Your ref: JJL/CS/Septimus
             Cooper/1351943-1

You continue to ask about the steps taken to refund other customers. Again you are only instructed by Mr Cooper. Notwithstanding, our client has confirmed that refunds will be made. If you now elect to issue court proceedings we shall refer the court to this correspondence where it has been made clear that refunds will be made.

Our reference to the term "reasonable endeavours" is taken from the OFGEM guidance. That provides that where there has been an overcharge the reseller must use reasonable endeavours to refund the whole amount of that overcharge.

In relation to interest, and again you are instructed only by Mr Cooper, we refer you to our without prejudice correspondence of today's date.

We note that you will remove the word "purposefully" from the press release. You suggest that the balance of the press release will be amended to address the identity of the contracting party. If you mean by this to allege that Mr Morphet has received payments to which he is not entitled then we have explained the position above and deny the assertion made by you. To suggest that Mr Morphet has therefore received money to which he is not entitled will be wholly incorrect and our client reserves all rights accordingly if you make such a publication.

Your penultimate paragraph is illogical. You have incorrectly assumed that Fell End is owned and operated by Pure Leisure Group Limited. We have put you right on that. The press release clearly relates to, and makes comments on, the actions of the owner of Fell End caravan park. That is Mr Morphet. To that end we are clearly entitled to make comment concerning the effect of the press release on Mr Morphet.

Yours faithfully

Weightmans LLP

On Monday 2 July, our Liverpool office moved to 100 Old Hall Street, Liverpool, L3 9QJ. Main telephone 0845 073 9900. Main fax: 0845 073 9950. DX 718100 Liverpool 16

With reference to Weightman's letter of the 17th August 2012 in reply to J.L.'s letter of the 16th August 2012 I would make comment regarding Mr. Fox's statements therein as follows: I cannot agree with what Mr. Fox is alleged to have said. A total untruthful concoction, utterly irrelevant to the reason for our meeting. Did I not know he was a director of Pure Leisure Group Ltd? So why should he invent all this? For the sake of lending weight to Weightman's defence, perhaps.

With reference to Weightman's opening paragraph of their second page I became aware of one particular "refund" when the recipient handed me a statement from Pure Leisure. A credit to his electric account of £600.00 plus was present, but without any breakdown details e.g. dates, accrued interest. I happened to mention this lump sum would be doing him financially more good if it was in *his* bank – after all it was *his* money! (this unsatisfactory state of affairs was probably bestowed on *all* other residents affected by the fraud). He duly visited the Pure Leisure Group Ltd. at their head office. Thereupon he obtained a cheque. Upon asking what was the reason for the refund he was informed "it was an overcharging caused by a computer glitch". You'll know the definition of this word – "a sudden irregularity". I would suggest that bizarre and outlandish statements such as these could sound the death-knell of our nationally known quip – "you couldn't make it up".

Weightmans

Liverpool L3 9QJ
DX 718100 Liverpool 16
www.weightmans.com

Irwin Mitchell
DX 14368
Manchester 1

Contact: Tom Collins
T: 0151 242 6939
E: tom.collins@weightmans.com

Our ref: MGR TCO LHE 445876 4
Your ref: JIL/CS/Septimus Cooper/1351943-1

By DX and fax: 0161 839 9804

17 August 2012

Dear Sirs

Without prejudice save as to costs
Re: Dispute with Septimus Cooper

We refer to your letter dated 16 August 2012.

Please note that the offer as set out on behalf of our client to yours in a letter dated 13 July 2012 and as reiterated in our letter dated 15 August 2012 is now hereby withdrawn and is incapable of acceptance.

Our client now makes a further offer. That offer is not made pursuant to Part 36. The offer is a global offer in full and final settlement of any and all claims between our respective clients inclusive of costs, interest, expenses, VAT and disbursements. It is an offer to pay to your client the sum of £7,500 in addition to the refund to be made of £1,201.53 to be subject to confidentiality (with the form or words to be agreed) and on condition that the press release to which you referred in your letter of 8 August 2012 (prepared on instruction from your client) or any such similar press release or publicity is not published. In the event that the press release or similar is so published then the offer shall be immediately withdrawn and will not be open for acceptance. In the event that your client accepts the offer but the press release or similar is then published then our client will commence proceedings against your client for recovery of the sum of £7,500 paid following your client's then breach of the terms of the offer. This offer remains open for acceptance for a period of 14 days, that is until 4pm on 31 August 2012.

In open correspondence you refer to the question of interest. Our client's offer accounts for interest.

Yours faithfully

Weightmans LLP

Irwinmitchell
solicitors

Your Ref: MGR TCO LHE 445876 4
Our Ref: JJL/CS/Sep Cooper/1394211-1

Weightmans LLP
Solicitors
DX 718100
LIVERPOOL 16

ALSO BY FAX: 0845 073 9950

20 August 2012

John Lord
john.lord@irwinmitchell.com
Tel: 0161 838 7276

Dear Sirs

Our Client: Septimus Cooper

Thank you for your letter dated 18 August 2012. 17TH ?

The "Company" website of Pure Leisure Group contains details of its registered office and also details the company number. The website advertises Fell End Caravan Park and the website is designed to cause visitors to the site to believe that the Company owns and operates all sites which are advertised. There is nothing whatsoever to link Mr Morphet to either the website or the Fell End Caravan Park. Indeed, the misrepresentation of the true position is carefully guarded by the Company, Mr Morphet and their agents. By way of example;

- Energy Cost Management claim to represent Pure Leisure Group but in fact they are representing Mr Morphet and the Company. On disclosure we would of course receive a copy of the relevant contract between Energy Cost Management and "Pure Leisure Group" and we very much doubt that Mr Morphet will be a contracting party.

- Mr Royle has corresponded with our client on the Company's registered notepaper.

Those who may be attracted to Fell End Caravan Park are likely to be attracted to the security which comes from contracting with a large company but of course, on your client's case they are not contracting with a large company at all. Perhaps you would care to explain why these misleading representations are being made to the public on the basis that the true position is likely to be highly material to the decision making process of those contemplating acquiring a caravan at the Fell End Caravan Park.

We have again considered the licence conditions and we think they are anything but "clear". Indeed, when we look at the web site, the correspondence and the position adopted by agents involved with the Park it seems to us that the contracting party is far more likely to be identified as the Company rather than Mr Morphet.

It appears to us that the Company and Mr Morphet are deliberately operating in a manner which is designed to misrepresent the identity of the contracting party. Our client believed that he was contracting with "the Company" and rightly assumed that a reputable company would not behave in a manner which would unlawfully seek to make a margin on electricity re-sold to its customers or serve an eviction notice for monies which were not owing. These actions did of course force our client to sell his caravan when he did not wish to do so.

167

We have the benefit of Mr Fox confirming that the only park exposed to this re-charging scandal is the Fell End Caravan Park. According to Mr Fox, the same or similar activities have not been undertaken at sites apparently owned and operated by the Company which perhaps highlights the basis for our client bringing an action founded upon a misrepresentation. We do not think that the Company can operate with impunity whilst being complicit in allowing Mr Morphet to position himself in a way which is designed to cause the public to believe that they are contracting with the Company rather than a sole trader. This is particularly the case here as Mr Morphet has over an extended period deliberately (and purposefully) re-sold electricity at a profit so as to enable an upgrade to his caravan park and thereby avoid personally footing the bill. This conduct has not been replicated by the Company which our client believed he was contracting with. Mr Fox has been understandably keen to distance himself from this conduct now that it is in the public arena.

We reserve our client's rights with respect to the identity of the contracting parties and we think the Company is in significant difficulties in light of its conduct and willingness to allow any reasonable observer to conclude that it owns and operates Fell End Caravan Park.

We accept that not all of the correspondence received by our client has been on the Company's notepaper but we do not think that will take you very far should the Court be asked to identify the contracting parties. Equally, your desire to focus on the discussions between Mr Fox and our client are entirely irrelevant to the contracting parties as this discussion took place years after the formation of the contract. A Court will look at the website, the wording of the licence, the absence of Mr Morphet's name on any document, the failure by Mr Morphet to fully and frankly disclose that he was a contracting party, and the marketing literature which is all designed to convey an impression that the Company owns the Fell End Caravan Park. The purpose of this seems to us to be in order that prospective customers believe they have the security of contracting with a reputable multi site operator. In our view, it is highly likely that a Court will find that the Company and our client were the contracting parties rather than our client and Mr Morphet.

We are of course happy to test these points especially as we think that the licence conditions also breach the Unfair Terms in Consumer Contracts Regulations 1994. The inability to properly identify the contracting parties undoubtedly strikes at the heart of the fairness principles but we feel that Clause 4 of the licence drives a coach and horses through the Regulations. We believe that your client and the Company ought to have serious concerns with respect to the oppressive nature of clause 4 which in our view will be successfully challenged at some point.

We now turn to the issue of the refunds. When will refunds be made? What steps has your client taken to make those refunds? Why has our client not received his refund? Please provide us with a cheque by return.

We note your reference to referring our correspondence to the Court. We doubt that there will be any reasons for you to do this as our correspondence will be attached to the proceedings should the refund fail to be made by return.

We consider that the OFGEM guidance to which you refer does not take into account a deliberate strategy of overcharging customers in order to avoid footing the bill for improvements. In the circumstances, we consider your client has a positive obligation to use his best endeavours to return trust money held for the benefit of others. We again invite your client to confirm how he intends to discharge his obligations to all users of the Park.

We have already confirmed that we are happy to remove the word "purposefully" from the press release even though the release, as drafted, accurately reflects your client's conduct. Mr Morphet has of course received money to which he is not entitled because he has received payments based on his inflated invoices and he has done nothing to return the sums which have been paid as a consequence of overcharging. Does Mr Morphet seek to assert that he has some kind of interest in such sums? If he does, please set out details of any interest which he feels he has. If he does not assert an interest in the overpayments then he is holding monies to which he has no entitlement. Whilst you may not be familiar with the defences which arise in defamation proceedings we think that "truth, fair comment and justification" would be difficult defences for Mr Morphet to overcome in the circumstances. That said, we are amending the press release and shall provide a copy to you in the hope that it may be approved by you in advance of publication.

We are interested in the relationship between Mr Morphet and the Company as it appears that the Company is integral to the running of the Fell End Caravan Park and the commercial relationship needs to be explored in greater detail. Would you care to advise us upon the details of this commercial relationship at this stage? We assume that the Company charges Mr Morphet for the services which it provides to him and Mr Morphet pays the Company to allow him to advertise his park on its website. Please clarify the nature of the commercial relationship as this issue is likely to be relevant to the contractual position.

Finally, please confirm whether Mr Morphet has, as yet, advised HMRC of the decision to apply a 5% VAT charge instead of a 17.5% or 20% VAT charge for services provided to Park users. If he has, please confirm the date when HMRC was notified of the error.

We look forward to hearing from you.

Yours faithfully

IRWIN MITCHELL LLP

Weightmans

Weightmans LLP
100 Old Hall Street
Liverpool L3 9QJ

T +44(0)845 073 9900
F +44(0)845 073 9950
DX 718100 Liverpool 16
www.weightmans.com

Irwin Mitchell
DX 14368
Manchester 1

Contact: Tom Collins
T: 0151 242 6939
E: tom.collins@weightmans.com

Our ref: MGR TCO LHE 445876 4
Your ref: JJL/CS/Septimus Cooper/1351943-1

BY FAX: 0161 839 9804

4 September 2012

Dear Sirs

Without prejudice save as to costs
Re: Dispute with Septimus Cooper

We refer to your letter dated 20 August 2012.

Your client has now been sent the refund cheque in the sum of £1,201.53.

So far as the confidentiality provisions are concerned we propose the following wording:

"The parties undertake to keep the terms of this agreement in the strictest confidence and they shall not disclose them to any other party except where there is agreement by all the parties in writing, disclosure is required by law and/or disclosure is made to the parties professional advisors including legal representatives for the purposes of obtaining legal advice on the terms of the agreement."

We then refer to your further letter dated 29 August 2012 concerning the press release. You are aware of the terms of our client's offer. Kindly confirm for the avoidance of doubt that your client has instructed you to issue the press release?

We look forward to hearing from you by return.

Yours faithfully

Weightmans

Weightmans LLP

COPY

Your Ref: MGR TCO LHE 445876 4
Our Ref: JJL/S5W/BLS-COMLIT/1427341-1

Weightmans LLP
Solicitors
DX 718100
LIVERPOOL 16

ALSO BY FAX: 0845 073 9950

29 August 2012

John Lord
john.lord@irwinmitchell.com
Tel: 0161 838 7276

Dear Sirs

Our Client: Septimus Cooper

We have reviewed the draft press release and believe that the following additions should be made:

"Correspondence between Irwin Mitchell and Weightmans, who have been appointed by Pure, has recently led to a claim that John Morphet is the owner of Fell End Caravan Park, despite the park being advertised on the web site of Pure Leisure Group Ltd. Mr Cooper has also received correspondence on Pure Leisure Group's notepaper from the Group Solicitor and Company Secretary, Mr Chris Royle with such correspondence also bearing Pure Leisure's company number. There remains a question as to whether Mr Cooper entered into contractual relations with the company or Mr Morphet, whose name does not appear on any of the documents provided to Mr Cooper. Mr Cooper states "I always believed that I was in a contract with a large reputable company but now I am being told that the owner of the site is actually Mr Morphet. I would question why neither the Pure Leisure Group website or any of the documents sent to me make this clear but irrespective of who owns the park, they have been overcharging their customers for electricity over an extended period in breach of OFGEM guidelines. I would suggest that anybody using the Fell End Caravan Park should give consideration to who they are contracting with and insist that the other contracting party be clearly identified.""

We are of course happy to remove the word "purposefully" even though we feel that the word is entirely accurate and fails to constitute a defamation by innuendo.

We look forward to receiving your response to this letter and our letter dated 20 August 2012.

Yours faithfully

IRWIN MITCHELL LLP

weightmans

Liverpool L3 9QJ
DX 718100 Liverpool 16
www.weightmans.com

Irwin Mitchell
DX 14368

Contact: Tom Collins

T: 0151 242 6939
E: tom.collins@weightmans.com

Our ref: MGR TCO CMH 445876 4
Your ref: JJL/CS/Septimus Cooper/1351943-1

BY FAX: 0161 839 9804

4 September 2012

Dear Sirs

Re: Dispute with Septimus Cooper

We refer to your letter dated 20 August 2012.

Again, we reiterate that you are instructed solely by Mr Cooper. To that end you will note that Mr Cooper has been paid a refund. You will also note that we have written to you on a without prejudice basis.

In the circumstances we fail to see on what basis you say you are entitled to any further information concerning any other party.

We confirm, for the avoidance of all doubt, that the contracting parties are the relevant park user and Mr Morphet.

So far as concerns the press release this is not agreed and our client does not give his approval to it. The fact of the matter is that, first, your client has been paid his refund and we therefore question on whose instruction you are sending the press release. Secondly, your client makes certain claims about the ownership of Fell End. Those claims are disputed. What you are seeking to do, and on whose instruction it is not clear, is to litigate those matters by way of a press release. That is inappropriate. If you elect to publish the press release notwithstanding then our client reserves all rights accordingly.

With regards to referring correspondence to the Court it is clear that (1) our client has confirmed that refunds will be made (2) your client has received a refund; and (3) any proceedings which are issued seeking to claim costs will be defended on the basis that it has been made clear that refunds will be made such that any claim for costs shall fail.

Yours faithfully

Weightmans LLP

Your Ref: MGR TCO CMH 445876 4
Our Ref: JJL/S5W/BLS-COMLIT/1446323-1

Weightmans LLP
Solicitors
DX: 718100
LIVERPOOL 16

VIA FAX (0)845 073 9950 AND DX

04 September 2012

John Lord
john.lord@irwinmitchell.com
Tel: 0161 838 7276

Dear Sirs

SECOND LETTER

Our Client: Septimus Cooper

Thank you for your letter dated 4 September 2012.

We confirm that at present we are only instructed by Mr Cooper.

Your client has charged and retained money to which he is not entitled. We have a duty to bring these issues to the attention of various parties in order to ensure that your client does not profit from his wrongdoing. There is nothing wrong with the requests for information which have been made and we insist upon you providing us with a full response.

We note that you believe that the contracting parties are Mr Morphet and the relevant park users. We do not accept that assessment as the contractual documents do not support that position. Our client considers that he contracted with Pure Leisure Group Ltd rather than Mr Morphet.

You have not clarified what issues your client has with the proposed press release. Please do so. Our client is entitled to provide a fair account of what has happened and you are in no position to prevent him from recounting his unhappy experiences to the press. For the avoidance of doubt, it is our client rather than us who will be speaking with the press and whilst your question with respect to on "whose instruction are you sending the press release" misses the point in spectacular fashion, the fact remains that our client can and will disclose to the press the rather distasteful and unlawful events which have taken place.

The claims with respect to Fell End seem to be disputed but you do not elaborate as to why this might be the case. Please clarify your client's objections to the draft press release/amend the press release for our consideration.

We are not seeking to litigate matters by way of a press release and this is a preposterous suggestion. Our client is conscious of his civic duty and rightly believes that the public should be warned about the Pure Leisure Group/Mr Morphet and Fell End. Our client intends to draw attention to the matters highlighted so that others are not placed in a similar invidious position at the hands of your client or the Pure Leisure Group and he is perfectly entitled to raise a newsworthy story of this nature with consumer rights groups as well as the national press.

Please confirm that every person affected by your client's unlawful conduct have now received a refund.

Too late in the day now but looking back on the issue of "who owns what?" it is glaringly obvious this was never resolved. Perhaps the trees had prevented both John Lord and I from seeing the wood.

Weightmans

Weightmans LLP
100 Old Hall Street
Liverpool L3 9QJ

T +44(0)845 073 9900
F +44(0)845 073 9950
DX 718100 Liverpool 16
www.weightmans.com

COPY

Irwin Mitchell
DX 14368
Manchester 1

Contact: Tom Collins

T: 0151 242 6939
E: tom.collins@weightmans.com

Our ref: MGR TCO GBE 445876 4
Your ref: JIL/CS/Septimus Cooper/1351943-1

By Fax: 0161 839 9804

6 September 2012

Dear Sirs

Your client: Septimus Cooper

We refer to your second letter dated 4 September 2012.

Thank you for confirming that you are only instructed by Mr Cooper. It is not accepted that, following such confirmation, you have a duty to bring the issues in question to the attention of "*various parties*". Our client has no obligation to provide any further information to you. However, your client has been refunded as have other park users.

We reiterate our earlier comments in relation to the press release. Our client does not give his agreement to it. It leaves an impression of Pure Leisure/Mr Morphet which is negative and unjustified.

Yours faithfully

Weightmans

Weightmans LLP

Weightmans

Liverpool L3 9QJ
DX 718100 Liverpool 16
www.weightmans.com

COPY

Irwin Mitchell
DX 14368
Manchester 1

Contact: Tom Collins
T: 0151 242 6939
E: tom.collins@weightmans.com

Our ref: MGR TCO GBE 445876 4
Your ref: JJL/CS/Septimus Cooper/1351943-1

By Fax: 0161 839 9804

6 September 2012

Dear Sirs

Without prejudice save as to costs
Re: Septimus Cooper

We refer to previous correspondence.

You will note that our client's offer expired on 31 August 2012. Notwithstanding, and in light of the fact that the proposed confidentiality wording was sent thereafter, our client is prepared to reopen that offer for a further 14 days.

That means that the offer made by way of our letter dated 17 August 2012 is now restated save that the confidentiality provisions shall be slightly amended to read

"The parties undertake to keep the existence of and the terms of this agreement in the strictest confidence and they shall not disclose it or them to any other party except where there is agreement by all the parties in writing, disclosure is required by law and/or disclosure is made to the parties professional advisors including legal representatives for the purposes of obtaining legal advice on the terms of the agreement."

The offer remains open for acceptance for a period of 14 days, that is until 4.00pm on 20 September 2012, following which it shall be withdrawn. We remind you again of the terms of the offer in relation to publication of the press release.

Now that we have responded to your open correspondence and you have this letter our client will not enter into any further correspondence save awaiting your client's instructions on the offer.

Yours faithfully

Weightmans LLP

Weightmans

100 Old Hall Street
Liverpool L3 9QJ

DX 718100 Liverpool 16
www.weightmans.com

Irwin Mitchell
DX 14368
Manchester 1

Contact: Sarah Conroy

T: 0151 242 6818
E: sarah.conroy@weightmans.com

Our ref: MGR SRX GBE 445876 4
Your ref: JJL/CS/Septimus Cooper/1351943-1

By Fax: 0161 839 9804 and DX

21 September 2012

Dear Sirs

Your client: Septimus Cooper
Without prejudice save as to costs
Subject to contract

We refer to your letter dated 17 September 2012 and note your client's counter offer of £10,000 in full and final settlement of the issues in dispute.

We confirm our client is agreeable to making a payment of £10,000 in settlement of the matter, subject to your client's acceptance of the terms of the enclosed draft Settlement Agreement.

We look forward to receiving your confirmation that the terms are agreed.

Yours faithfully

Weightmans LLP

Weightmans LLP

Enclosure: Draft Settlement Agreement

Irwin Mitchell
solicitors

Your Ref: MGR TCO LHE 445876 4
Our Ref: JJL/CS/BLS-COMLIT/1511408-1

Weightmans LLP
Solicitors
DX 718100
LIVERPOOL 16

24 September 2012

ALSO BY FAX: 0845 073 9950

John Lord
john.lord@irwinmitchell.com
Tel: 0161 838 7276

WITHOUT PREJUDICE SAVE AS TO COSTS

SUBJECT TO CONTRACT

Dear Sirs

Our Client: Septimus Cooper

Thank you for your letter dated 21 September 2012.

We have reviewed the draft Agreement. Clause 2(b) is clearly not a term which should ever be in the contemplation of the parties. This dispute has been ongoing for over 5 years. During that time, our client has instructed 2 firms of solicitors, discussed matters extensively with members of OFGEM and other officials and discussed matters with his family and friends. Our client has agreed to a confidentiality clause and the additional terms expressed in correspondence. Our client self evidently cannot agree to a clause which fails to appreciate the nature of the dispute, the longevity of the dispute, the work undertaken by our client to establish liability and the natural consequences of having friends and family who have been concerned by the impact which the dispute has had on our client's health.

We also consider it appropriate to state within the compromise agreement that Mr Royle, Pure's Group Company Secretary identified the issues relevant to the profit generated by your client as a re-seller in his correspondence with our client.

Further, 2(d) is obviously not going to be acceptable. If your client is able to establish breach to the satisfaction of the Court then your client will get an order entitling him to repayment.

We request that clauses 2(b) and 2(d) be removed, the involvement of Mr Royle be added to the recitals and that amendments be made to 2(c) in recognition of the fact that 2(b) fails to appreciate the reality of the position. Assuming that your client genuinely wishes to resolve this dispute now, we cannot imagine that the demanded changes are in any way controversial.

We look forward to hearing from you.

Yours faithfully

IRWIN MITCHELL LLP

Liverpool L3 9QJ   DX 718100 Liverpool 16
                       www.weightmans.com

Irwin Mitchell
DX 14368
Manchester 1

Manchester Post Room
03 OCT 2012

Contact: Sarah Conroy
T: 0151 242 6818
E: sarah.conroy@weightmans.com

Our ref: MGR SBX GBE 445876 4
Your ref: JJL/CS/Septimus Cooper/1351943-1

By Fax: 0161 839 9804 and DX

2 October 2012

Dear Sirs

Your client: Septimus Cooper
Without prejudice save as to costs
Subject to contract

We refer to your letter dated 24 September 2012.

We note your comments in respect of clause 2(b) and have amended this to reflect the fact that the written confirmation shall relate to future notifications only. We trust that this will not be an issue for Mr Cooper given the terms of the confidentiality provisions.

In respect of clause 2(d) you will appreciate that your client has indicated on a number of occasions that he intends to issue a press release about the matters in dispute. Our client is concerned that your client will proceed to issue a press release whether directly or through a third party and accordingly we have amended clause 2(d) to reflect our client's concerns in that respect.

We note your comments in respect of Mr Royle, however, we do not consider that this is relevant for inclusion in the agreement.

We now look forward to receiving your client's signed agreement so that the matter can be brought to a close.

Yours faithfully

Weightmans LLP

Weightmans LLP

Enclosure: Draft Settlement Agreement

Irwin Mitchell
solicitors

Your Ref: MGR TCO LHE 445876 4
Our Ref: JJL/CS/Sep Cooper/1542128-1

Weightmans LLP
Solicitors
DX 718100
LIVERPOOL 16

3 October 2012

ALSO BY FAX: 0845 073 9950

John Lord
john.lord@irwinmitchell.com
Tel: 0161 838 7276

WITHOUT PREJUDICE SAVE AS TO COSTS

Dear Sirs

Our Client: Septimus Cooper

Thank you for your letter dated 2 October 2012.

2(b) is actually superfluous to requirements because our client is bound by 2(a). 2(a) deals with future notification of the dispute so what is the point of 2(b) when your client already has the benefit conferred under the agreement?

We cannot help but feel that you are seeking to over engineer the compromise and all that is happening is that legal costs are escalating.

2(c) needs to be amended to remove reference to 2(b). 2(d) needs amending because the settlement agreement can be disclosed but not the terms of settlement and again, the clause as drafted would prevent our client from confirming the dispute has been settled (which we would have thought your client would not have any objection to).

Equally 2(d) would necessitate your client evidencing that our client was responsible. You cannot seriously expect our client to pay your client upon receipt of a demand by your client. Indeed, why are we even arguing about this issue? If our client breaches and your client establishes breach before a Court then he will be entitled to damages to the value of the sums paid.

Please amend and let us have a copy of the agreement in Word so that we may amend the next draft should it require further amendment.

Yours faithfully

IRWIN MITCHELL LLP

www.weightmans.com

Irwin Mitchell
DX 14368
Manchester 1

Contact: Sarah Conroy
T: 0151 242 6818
E: sarah.conroy@weightmans.com

Our ref: MGR SBX CMH 445876 4
Your ref: JJL/CS/Septimus Cooper/1351943-1

By Fax: 0161 839 9804 and DX

17 October 2012

Dear Sirs

Your client: Septimus Cooper
Without prejudice save as to costs
Subject to Contract

We refer to your letter dated 15 October 2012.

Our position remains as previously advised; our client is prepared to agree to the removal of clause 2b, however, 2d is required to remain as drafted.

We note your comments in respect of our client serving written notification on spurious grounds, however, the clause is quite clear that it relates to the issue by your client; or the procuring by a third party of a press release about the dispute and/or the terms or existence of the settlement agreement.

The clause is precise and can only be acted upon by our client where such a press release is made. We do not consider that there is any risk of our client serving notification on spurious grounds and are concerned by the level of resistance which your client is mounting to the incorporation of this clause. We repeat that if it is your client's intention to comply with the confidentiality provisions, we do not see that the inclusion of this clause as drafted in the settlement agreement should present a problem.

We are not prepared to correspond further on the matter and look forward to receiving confirmation that the terms are agreed, following which payment of the £10,000 can be made.

Yours faithfully

Weightmans LLP

Realising you have just read the legal exchanges between the two company solicitors I will restrain myself and keep my comments as limited as my conscience will allow. You will have noted the Mr. Collins of Weightmans (W) in his opening letter of the 15th August 2012, right from the word go made the following statement: "We make it clear the overcharging was an innocent error". This comment coming from a man representing the very backbone of British justice. Had he got mixed up with another case? A man who probably charges more for two hours of his work than the average paid employee earns in a week. To me, I believe his audacious and reckless remark was borne out by the fact he's been given charge of acting in defence of the indefensible: and he knew it. Did you notice the number of times (W) referred to the word press release. Twenty-four, in fact. It lends belief to his client's desperation in having this course of action suffocated. Even fearful, perhaps? Never. W not once used the words "wrongful eviction" which represented part of my claim. They preferred the word "losses". A sad, sly way of hiding the sordid, corrupt and shameful truth of the matter.

As an aside I wonder if, like me, you have found it interesting to see that almost each and every letter from Weightmans begins with the words "We *refer* to your letter...". As opposed to Irwin Mitchell's wording "*Thank you* for your letter..."

John Lord has since left Irwin Mitchell. He is now a senior partner with:

T.L.T. Solicitors,
3, Hardman Street
Manchester
M3 3EB

Email. johnlord@tltsolicitors.com
Kindly find herein the complete text of the agreement.

Dated _____ 2012

(1) JOHN MORPHET T/A PURE LEISURE

(2) SEPTIMUS COOPER

AGREEMENT

Weightmans LLP
100 Old Hall Street
Liverpool L3 9QJ

THIS AGREEMENT is dated   2012 and is made

BETWEEN:

(1) JOHN MORPHET T/A PURE LEISURE of South Lakeland House, Yealand, Redmayne, Carnforth, Lancashire LA5 9RM ("JM"); and

(2) SEPTIMUS COOPER of [insert address details] ("SC")

together known as the "Parties".

RECITALS

WHEREAS

(A) JM and SC entered into an agreement in or around 2006 in respect of the siting of SC's caravan at Fell End Caravan Park ("the Site"), owned by JM. As part of that agreement electricity charges in respect of the supply of electricity to SC's caravan were payable by SC within 14 days of demand;

(B) On 16 February 2012 SC's representatives notified Pure Leisure Group/ Pure Leisure Limited/JM of alleged overcharging in respect of the electricity charges contrary to the relevant guidelines provided by OFGEM;

(C) SC further alleged that to the extent the overcharges related to improvements to the Site's utilities that JM had incorrectly treated the VAT to be applied to those improvements;

(D) Further, SC subsequently sold his caravan on the Site. SC raised a dispute concerning the circumstances surrounding his departure from the Site and the sale of his caravan to JM as detailed in the correspondence exchanged between the Parties and their advisers;

(E) SC has alleged that the issues detailed above involve JM, Pure Leisure Group Limited and Pure Leisure ("the Dispute").

The Parties have agreed to settle the Dispute as expressly provided for in this Agreement without the admission of liability by either party.

NOW IT IS HEREBY AGREED AS FOLLOWS:

1. JM agrees to pay the sum of £10,000 (ten thousand pounds) ("the Settlement Sum") to SC by [ ] with such sum to be paid in full and final settlement of the Dispute, any underlying facts relating to the Dispute, whether as set out in correspondence between the respective legal advisors for JM and SC or otherwise and any and all causes of action, claims, demands or otherwise of whatever nature whether known about or unknown which the Parties have or may have against each other arising out of or in connection with the Dispute including but not limited to claims for costs, interest, VAT, damages, expenses and disbursements.

2. (a) The Parties undertake to keep the existence of and terms of the Agreement and the Dispute in the strictest confidence and they shall not disclose the existence of or the terms of this Agreement and the Dispute to any other party whatsoever except where there is agreement by all the Parties in writing, disclosure is required by law and/or disclosure is made to the Parties' professional advisers including legal representatives for the purposes of obtaining legal advice on the terms of the Agreement or as is necessary to enforce the terms of the Agreement; and

    (b) It is a condition precedent to payment of the Settlement Sum that SC shall provide written confirmation by no later than 14 days from the date of this Agreement that no prior notification of the subject matter of the Dispute has been provided to any third party and that there will be no future notification of the subject matter of the Dispute to any third party, save for the excepted parties detailed at Clause 2(a) above; and

    (c) For the avoidance of any doubt, the confidentiality provisions detailed at Clauses 2(a) and (b) apply to any disclosure of the subject matter of the Dispute to a third party in respect of JM, Pure Leisure and Pure Leisure Group Limited, save for the exceptions detailed therein.

    (d) In the event of a breach of the confidentiality provisions detailed at clause 2(a) of this Agreement SC agrees to repay the Settlement Sum in its entirety as a debt due and owing to JM within 14 days of written notification of the breach by JM or his advisers and in the event that SC does not make such repayment JM shall be entitled to recover the Settlement Sum from SC as a debt.

5. This Agreement contains the entire agreement between the Parties in relation to the subject matter of the Dispute. The Parties irrevocably and unconditionally waive any right each may have to claim damages for and/or to rescind this Agreement because of breach of any warranty not expressly contained in this Agreement or any misrepresentation whether or not contained in this Agreement unless such misrepresentation was made fraudulently.

6. This Agreement and any dispute or claim arising out of, relating to or in connection with it is governed by English law and is subject to the exclusive jurisdiction of the English Courts to which the Parties irrevocably submit.

We, the undersigned, hereby agree to the terms stated in this Agreement.

SIGNED by JOHN MORPHET T/A PURE LEISURE) Signed: ....

Print Name: ....

DATED: ....

SIGNED by SEPTIMUS COOPER) Signed: ....

DATED: ....

of breach of any warranty not expressly contained in this Agreement or any misrepresentation whether or not contained in this Agreement unless such misrepresentation was made fraudulently.

6. This Agreement and any disputes or claim arising out of, relating to or in connection with it is governed by English law and is subject to the exclusive jurisdiction of the English Courts to which the Parties irrevocably submit.

We, the undersigned, hereby agree to the terms stated in this Agreement.

SIGNED by JOHN MORPHET T/A PURE LEISURE) Signed: *J.C. Morphet*

DATED:

SIGNED by SEPTIMUS COOPER) Signed: *S Cooper*

DATED:

23. THE REAL ELECTRIC FRAUD – THE COMPLETE TRUTH OF THE MATTER?

Mr. Royle (viz the Pure Leisure Group) fell on his sword due to his fatal letter, to my solicitors of the 14th February 2011. The reasons given in this letter for their year ending 2008 charge rate became the focal point of Mr. John Lord's attack, from which Mr. Royle's virtually non-existent defence collapsed. However the latter obviously believed his explanations would serve the purpose of totally deceiving all and sundry.

From the outset it hit home to me that the yearly dates and their respective contractual charges laid out by Energy Cost Management in their letter of 16th April 2009 had been blatantly altered by P.L.G. i.e. the 12.63p per unit prince for the year ending 2009 had deliberately been brought forward by one year, thus replacing the 2008 contracted unit price of 7.06p. An increase of over 75%. It is there in black and white for all to see. It was done in such a simplistic way, but with what potentially devastating results. Mr. Royle's electric system repairs and renewals explanation for the overcharging was a complete and desperate red herring. A malicious (and what he thought clever) deception designed to take one off the scent. To side-track. To mislead. Regretted by me to this day and although in full agreement with my appraisal as to the truth of the matter my solicitor would only go down the road where absolute proof was to hand. I personally knew we had this proof. About this time national electric prices were rising, no more so than in 2008. You will recall in suffering that year's very big hike. 30% plus? This would, I believe, encourage any fraudulent thoughts the Fell End Park management were having – strike now, under the cover of the electric giants far more than average increases (especially 2008). Use these as a smoke-screen. In the belief they had 'got away with it' overcharging was still taking place, up to and including the year 2011.

A sign that over the years they had indoctrinated or indeed unknowingly radicalized themselves knowing that they could do anything, especially in the interests of profit, and escape conviction. A sick culture had developed. I had also become aware Fell End's fraudulent activities were being levied on two of their other nearby parks.

South Lakeland Leisure Village and Hall More Parks are two of several sites owned by Pure Leisure Group Ltd. throughout the United Kingdom. They are situated approximately four miles and one mile from the Fell End Park respectively.

I confidentially informed Mr. William Huxley, a Hall More resident, of my growing concerns regarding the electricity overcharging at Fell End and wondered if this fraud could be taking place at the Hall More site where he resided. He duly checked his past invoices wherein it was discovered the electric rate charged during the years in question virtually matched those of mine. I kept Bill in touch as to my progress but when the time was ripe he, obviously armed with the information etc. provided by me, visited the Pure Leisure Group's head office and duly received a refund. He didn't have to make me aware of his actions but he has not communicated with me in any shape or form – even to this very day. It came to my knowledge that another lady resident had also received a refund (my mole was continuing to do a good job).

Some of us may recall the war-time slogan: "walls have ears". A South Lakeland Leisure Village resident, Mr. Barry Thorpe, who probably couldn't help overhearing my remarks regarding the overcharging, later approached me explaining his serious concern regarding the situation where he resided. To cut a long story short when, some considerable time later, as I thought we were making good progress basically in his interests, he abruptly and in my humble view rudely interrupted my verbal flow and said, and I quote, "I don't want to go into it Sep" and then the line went dead. I've never heard from him since.

As with Bill Huxley, I remain baffled as to their parallel actions, or lack of same. The main point in all this however, is that it proved to me that residents of other parks, contrary to Pure Leisure's denial to this day, were falling foul of their overcharging scandal. Those of you with a more imaginative mind than I could well see the reason for this "common-denominator conundrum".

You will not have failed to observe that Mr. Royle is the principle cheat in the practical arranging of both the electrical fraud and its attempted cover-up. In this connection, two points (facts) well worth noting are as follows:

1. He possesses the business title of *Group* Solicitor and Company Secretary.
2. The electric needs of *all* the Pure Leisure Group sites, in addition to Fell End Caravan Park, are supplied by Energy Cost Management, with whom the Fell End Park management appear to enjoy a very cosy relationship.
3. Despite the foregoing he *surely* would have had to keep the P.L.G. hierarchy fully informed all times of the fraud's progress?

24. E.O.N.

At this late juncture I bring in the electric suppliers whom Energy Cost Management deal with. They go under the banner of E.O.N.. Enclosed herein are two copy letters to this German company from the writer, which you will find self-explanatory.

E.O.N. did not reply to my last two missives. Regrettably I did not pursue the matter as it did not directly concern the Fell End Caravan Park. However, the park is all part of the mix and I could not waste or resist this opportunity to bring to light the questionable attitude of a large, international company when posed with difficult questions when regarding their integrity. Questions they chose to ignore.

I will leave you to form *your* opinions as to whether they did or did not take action to remedy anything untoward as outlined in my correspondence. By not replying this leaves them at least open to question regarding the quality of their dealings which ultimately affect the finances of the general public who, after all, are their customers and their main source of income.

The least I can do, if possible, is to send the two forementioned dealers in electricity a signed copy of this book.

1 St. Anthony's Close
Milnthorpe
Cumbria
LA7 7DT

Tel No 01539 64053

24th September 2013

FTAO Mr Mark Redmond
EON
Westwood Way
Westwood Business Park
Coventry
CV4 8LG

Dear Sir,

RE: ENERGY COST MANAGEMENT (ECM) & PURE LEISURE GROUP LTD PLG

May I please have a reply to my letter of the 29th August 2013?
I would remind you of your promise of the 5th August to write to me.
Failing receipt of your reply to this letter within ten days leaves me with no option but to pursue the matter elsewhere.

Yours sincerely

Mr Septimus Cooper

1 St Anthony's Close
Milnthorpe
Cumbria
LA7 7DT

Tel No: 015395 64053

29th August 2013

FAO Mark Redmond
EON
Westwood Way
Westwood Business Park
Coventry
CV4 8LG

Dear Mr Redmond

RE: ENERGY COST MANAGEMENT (ECM) & PURE LEISURE GROUP LTD (PLG)

With reference to our telephone conversation of the 5th inst, your promise to write to me has not materialised?

The file I supplied to you shows, without doubt, ECM (Agents of PLG?) are aware PLG have been overcharging, e.g. PLG increased their rate to 12.63 in 2008 when in fact ECM charged them 7.06kwh. ECM are aware of this – an increase of 76.5%!

It could be construed that if EON now continue to have dealings with ECM/PLG, they are not distancing themselves from corruption. One could not be blamed for believing EON has at least a moral and civic duty to abide by and as such should stand by these principles and take the appropriate action.

A reply would be appreciated.

Yours sincerely

Septimus Cooper

25. OH! THE SUPPLY OF GAS

The law of the land states: "A landlord cannot charge more for gas or electricity than they have paid for it".

It is known as the maximum retail price and applies if you "own or rent a caravan and buy gas or electricity from the owner"

Fell End Park operated a gas bottle system. I was unsuccessful in my efforts to obtain what price the park had been paying their suppliers during the years relevant to me. It was no co-incidence, however, that I was aware of several residents, like me, who purchased their bottled gas from an outlet several miles away from the park. There it was a great deal cheaper. The expense of the round trip was well worthwhile. The park management were well aware of these surreptitious movements. Surprisingly, and not in keeping with form, no action was ever taken by them to counteract these thrifty manoeuvres. Why? You may or may not wonder.

Finally it has now come to my knowledge that gas bottles are only available on Mondays, Wednesdays and Fridays. They must also be ordered before the previous Saturday. Convenient or inconvenient? It depends whose side you are on.

26. CONSCIENCE AND CIVIC DUTY

Having read the inter-solicitor correspondence you will have observed my taking of the overcharging amount (£1,201.53) and the compensation amount (£10,000). The latter follows offers from the Pure Leisure Group of £3/4,000 - £5,000 - £7,500 and £10,000. This final offer I accepted, and as previously stated, with unease. Firstly I had to sign a confidentiality agreement and secondly this acceptance of the 'hush' monies was in total contradiction to any morals I might have had regarding conscience and civic duty. I had allowed these, in fact, to be swallowed up by putting monetary gain to the fore. A hypocrite if ever there was one. Mitigating circumstances I offer in the form of advice (pressure?) from my solicitor, my wife, my children, my friends and my tired brain – to accept and move on after this four and a half year battle, not good enough I know.

In mid-January 2013 I was enjoying a stroll in shirtsleeves order under the pleasant sun which Malta can provide at that time of the year. The only distraction to this blissful experience were my sad thoughts of two months earlier when I signed away what principles I had. Later, at dinner, I espied Fell End Park chums, Mr. and Mrs. Pollard. They owned a holiday home which was sited 'round the corner' from mine whilst we resided at Fell End Park: they told me they had left the site. Their departure being under the usual enforced terms left them feeling extremely disgruntled to say the least. Later it dawned on me this chance meeting was fate. I knew there and then that I had to re-trace my steps. I commenced carrying out this course of action by writing to Pure Leisure (after more deep and prolonged thought) in May 2013. Copies of the five self-explanatory letter interchanges, reference numbers 1 to 5 are herein shown. Pure Leisure's written refusal to accept return of my compensation amount contravenes in no uncertain manner the terms of the agreement. You will see repayment means that the provisions therein cease. This includes that of disclosure to any third party. Clause 20 confirms this. Indeed, this has since been confirmed by three unconnected company solicitors.

I thought of various ways of bringing the Pure Leisure Group's fraud and corruption into the public domain. This included the press, T.V. and the courts. I felt, however, that these actions would result in short-lived nine day wonders resulting in long-term maximum publicity not being achieved. Anything less would not be deserving of all those who have suffered at the hands of this caravan park's company. Ongoing referral availability to the scandal was what I needed. A book!

Left with no further option I decided to put pen to paper. But was I capable of this? I was comforted with the thought that some sixty years ago I had gained an 'A-Level' in English (or was it an 'O'?!). It took me until early November 2013 to commence writing. After putting off the start for four months – thinking only – I somehow developed a little willpower.

I re-iterate three independent firms of solicitors have all confirmed my legal obligations under the terms of the confidentiality agreement would cease upon the repayment of the settlement sum.

The decision made by Pure Leisure in their letter of the 23rd May 2013 served only to spur me on in 'going public' and to write the book.

1 St Anthony's Close
Milnthorpe
Cumbria
LA7 7DT

13th May 2013

Pure Leisure Group
A6, Yealand Redmayne
Carnforth
Lancashire
LA5 9RN

Dear Sirs

RE: CONFIDENTIALLITY AGREEMENT-JOHN MORPHET & SEPTIMUS COOPER

Since the above agreement came into force I am now led to believe that your fraudulent activities with regards to the electrical overcharging are on a far greater scale than those confined only to your Fell End Caravan Park.

In addition to this I, at this stage, have now given way to my civic duty responsibilities which will enforce me to consider making public your unlawful activities which would also include the following government authorities:

- HMRC
- OFGEM
- SFO
- OFT

EON, together with the local and national press, will also be furnished with the relevant parts of the correspondence which has passed between us and my solicitors over the past four and half years.

Would you therefore, let me have the sum you require to absolve me from all binding provisions contained in the foresaid agreement.

Yours truly

Septimus Cooper

1 St Anthony's Close

Milnthorpe

Cumbria

LA7 7DT

J C Morphet T/A Pure Leisure

South Lakeland House

Yealand Redmayne

Carnforth

LA5 9RM

23 May 2013

Dear Mr Cooper

Agreement

Thank you for your letter dated 13 May.

The agreement was entered into by both parties in good faith and we expect you to honour that agreement and we have no intention to relieve you of its binding provisions.

Yours sincerely

A M Fox

For and on behalf of J C Morphet T/A Pure Leisure

POSTED 1ST CLASS RECORDED DELIVERY – 21-05-13   226

Mr Septimus Cooper
1 St. Anthony's Close
Milnthorpe
Cumbria
LA7 7DT

31st May 2013

PURE LEISURE GROUP LTD
And Mr J C Morphet, T/A Pure Leisure
South Lakeland House
A6, Yealand Redmayne
Carnforth
Lancashire
LA5 9RN

Dear Sirs,

With reference to your letter of 23rd inst, I will now be proceeding with the actions as stated in my letter to you of 13th May 2013.

These actions will commence from the 19th June 2013, by which time I will be in possession of the complete picture surrounding your Group's electrical overcharging and also my wrongful eviction.

Yours truly

[signature: Cooper]

Mr Septimus Cooper

199

R 19.6.13

1 St Anthony's Close

Milnthorpe

Cumbria

LA7 7DT

J C Morphet T/A Pure Leisure

South Lakeland House

Yealand Redmayne

Carnforth

LA5 9RM

14 June 2013

Dear Mr Cooper

Agreement

Thank you for your letter dated 31 May.

We seem to have established that you understand the consequences of your proposed actions so there is little else I can add to this correspondence other than to say that we will of course take appropriate action ourselves should it become necessary.

Yours sincerely

A M Fox

For and on behalf of J C Morphet T/A Pure Leisure

1 St Anthony's Close
Milnthorpe
Cumbria
LA7 7DT

26th June 2013

Private & Confidential
PURE LEISURE GROUP LTD
And Mr J C Morphet, T/A Pure Leisure
6, Yealand Redmayne
Carnforth
Lancashire
LA5 9RN

Dear Sirs

With reference to your letter of 14th inst, I note what you have to say however, I will still be taking action as stated in my letter of 31st May 2013, and this will commence on or near to the 8th July 2013.

Yours truly

Mr Septimus Cooper

INTERLUDE – PAUSE FOR THOUGHT

A good part of my time spent in the realization of this book has taken place during 2014. If any, *the* year for remembering those who paid the ultimate sacrifice during the two world wars. We, who live on, should revere them, which includes showing this reverence throughout our daily working lives: in a manner which aims to give love, respect, fair-mindedness and honesty towards our fellow beings – as those heroes would have wished.

How is it, therefore, adult persons can be capable of perpetrating such on-going wrong-doings which openly disregard the hopes of all those who died? Thankfully they are in a tiny minority, otherwise could their devotion have been in vein?

P.s. I toured the Western Front in August 2014. This sombre experience rightly, wrongly or inappropriately compelled me to include these thoughts in the book.

MISCELLANY

In avoiding an over-indulgence in chapters and to ease my book towards a timely conclusion this ultimate chapter covers several stories, factual accounts and comments. I hope you will find they are just as worthy of inclusion as those gone before!

Enclosed herein are two copies of Fell End Park electrical invoices in connection with the years 2003 (A) and 2004 (B). They were kindly given to me by a fellow resident. You will be shocked (or will you?) to see that the "admin charge" appertaining to each averaged 17.78 pence per day. A cost in excess of the actual electricity consumed!

In comparison with Fell End's absurd figures the present supplier of my home's needs, E.D.F., contractually charge me for the years 2014/15 the sum of 18 pence per day. This, of course, is virtually the same figure charged by Fell End of ten years ago and equates to 17% of the gross amount. Not, as in in Fell End's case, an average charge of 119%.

South Lakeland Caravans
South Lakeland House
Yealand Redmayne
Nr. Carnforth
Lancs
LA5 9RN

REF. A

VAT REG Number 514 3195 67

Invoice

Invoice	9664
Tax Date	29/
Account No.	FW......

		Unit Price	Net Amount	VAT Amount
605.00	Units of Electricity used Previous - 3955 Present - 4560	0.0417	25.23	1.26
1.00	Admin Charge 1st February - 31st July 2003 6 months	32.5000	32.50	1.63

PLEASE SEND ALL PAYMENTS TO:-

FELL END CARAVAN PARK
Slackhead Road
Hale
Milnthorpe
LA7 7BS

Net Amount	57.73
VAT Amount	2.89
Carriage	0.00
Invoice Total	60.62

South Lakeland House
Yealand Redmayne
Nr. Carnforth
Lancs
LA5 9RN

REF. B.

VAT REG Number 514 3195 67

Invoice

Invoice	10480
Tax Date	31/01/
Account No.	FWH252

Quantity	Product Description	Unit Price	Net Amount	VAT Amount
746.00	Units of Electricity used Previous - 4560 Present - 5306	0.0400	29.84	1.49
1.00	Admin Charge 1st August 2003 - 31st January 2004 6 months	32.5000	32.50	1.63

PLEASE SEND ALL PAYMENTS TO:-

FELL END CARAVAN PARK
Slackhead Road
Hale
Milnthorpe
LA7 7BS

Net Amount	62.34
VAT Amount	3.12
Carriage	0.00
Invoice Total	65.46

Shown herein is a copy of a letter received from Mr. Andrew Eckersley, a Fell End Park resident, which is self-explanatory. In Andy's inimitable way it sums up the whole shebang in giving an example of one of the park's vicious mechanisms they would, and could, put into operation in defence of their interests. Andy is a 'reet grand' Lancashire lad with a heart of gold and a family to be proud of. He has given me the authority to publish his letter. Needless to say he never received a refund. He did receive however, quite some time after his missive to me, an eviction notice.

18/11/2012

Mr A S Eckersley

32 Calder Drive

Swinton

Manchester

M27 9SY

RE : Pure Leisure (Fell End) electricity over charging.

Dear Mr Cooper,

With reference to the above, we occupied pitch E and Pitch K for the past 5 years.

Please accept this letter as authority to act on my behalf in an effort to be refunded moneys overcharged.

Even though our caravan was touring, we paid for a twelve month pitch which we spent every weekend, also all the school holidays, our caravan was a hobby which the heating run on electric and was in a static position all year round, working out

1

some figures ive been overcharged between £600 - £800.

We did know at the time of the over charging, but because we had kids we did not want to be evicted from the campsite, which would happen if you approach management.

yours sincerley

Mr A S Eckersley

2

Towards the end of our tenure at Fell End, during a period lasting about thirty months, five site managers came and went. No doubt you will have gleaned by now they had, in effect, little or no authority. Four of the site managers were dismissed, apart from Eric who I mentioned earlier.

The story of John, one of the unfortunate four, I now recount as follows:

John was the established manager of a leading national gents' outfitters situated on the main shopping thoroughfare knows as Fishergate, in the centre of Preston, Lancs.. A position which no doubt promised a long and successful career. He was, however, enticed by Pure Leisure to take on the role of site manager at the Fell End caravan park. The enticement took a long time to succeed. John told me he'd refused to rise to the bait on numerous occasions. A rent free house on the park came with the job. He sold his home and moved with his wife and children to Fell End. In other words he uprooted, lock stock and barrel.

During his eleven months at Fell End I found him to be diligent, convivial and courteous at all times. He put into operation several park enhancing features, not least those of a health and safety nature.

Just prior to the opening of the new leisure complex, and one month before the completion of a year's service at the park his tenure came to an abrupt halt. This by way of termination of his employment and which carried no period of notice.

John and his wife had completely re-furbished the Park's house. This included new curtains and venetian blinds throughout, which went with the evictees retreat to Burnley.

The vacancy (if there ever was one) was filled almost immediately and coincided with the opening of the new leisure complex. The new site manager was a certain Mr. John Hurst.

I had occasion to contact an ex park resident of long-standing at his home who informed me he had left Fell End, and duly explained the reason for this. As requested by the Fell End management he agreed to clean the windows of the Park's leisure complex on a fortnightly basis with a cash payment promised on the completion of each stint. A jovial character, but not one to tangle with. He, having not received any payment for the second and third cleaning operations, paid a visit to the park's bar, called over the steward, who he then instructed to extract from the cash till the amount owed to him. This done, he lodged a receipt in the till together with a note advising those running the park of his feelings. Whilst no more was heard or said he told me this was the culmination of several unsavoury incidents he'd experienced, and the final straw.

During 2008, I discovered the Pure Leisure Group's head office had overcharged me in 2007 £70.00 (seventy pounds) in respect of V.A.T.. This was in connection with site fees. I duly paid the 2009 site fees, *less* the overcharge. Nothing has been said to this day regarding my deliberate "short-changing".

In an attempt to maximise the authenticity of the book I would have liked to "name names" in every instance, but with the realisation that some form of retribution could be enforced on those by Pure Leisure, for example those who are current residents, employees, local people etc., I have limited name disclosures to those directly responsible for creating the vile, despicable actions I have witnessed.

There is a strong possibility a legal onslaught will be instigated by the Fell End Park, i.e. Pure Leisure. So be it. The fact that my non-fiction book has reached the outside world and in turn your attention has made me more contented and a happier man than I have been for quite a number of years.

There is a saying out there "to remain silent is a crime". I would supplement this with "corruption survives and thrives on silence". This thought came to me and inspired me during the course of my writings.

I have taken more than a crumb of comfort from my hunch that if the Fell End Caravan Park is continuing to operate on the same lines as revealed in my book it will have no lasting future. Should its demise come about this in effect I suggest would put an end to a wretched situation festering in the caravan park industry – all to the good.

Long after my early uneasiness regarding the way residents were being treated I decided to keep a written record of any wrong-doings actuated by the park. This I kept in meticulous form. It accounted for all of the Fell End Park's actions of despicability which I became aware of. This chronicle became the factual source and provider of a good deal of information without which I would have lacked confidence in taking on the task ahead. Even so I needed encouragement. This was forthcoming to a degree when I took into my confidence a highly respected leading South Lakeland District Liberal Democrat councillor in early 2014. He was all too pleased to read my partly written account, which he duly returned with the following written, rather poignant statement.

This, to the letter, is as follows:
Septimus
A horror story by any stretch of the imagination. Steven King could not have written better. They have no regard for anybody. Is this the English Mafia!

You will have gathered that the owner of the Fell End Caravan Park is a sole trader carrying out this business under the title/name of Pure Leisure. Although not being at all au fait with the law regarding the trades description act it appears obvious to me, in view of the continuous bitter experiences perpetrated upon park residents that a definite contravention of this act has, at least in my time of residence, been taking place.

Viz. "Pure": meaning – chaste, guiltless, sincere, morally undefiled, uncorrupt

(The Oxford Dictionary – 1996)

It must be noted the revelations exposed herein are only tantamount to my personal experiences over a relatively short period of time (six years). The mind boggles at the thought of what the full twenty years or so would disclose i.e. since Pure Leisure's acquisition of Fell End Caravan Park. I reiterate, all these exposés have come to my knowledge despite being only one resident out of hundreds.

The following data gives some idea of the struggle my solicitors (2) and I experienced in reaching a conclusion to what became, no less, a saga. Needless to say we did our best to constantly hurry matters along but to no avail! Me – 28th October 2008 to 6th July 2010 – 20 months. Solicitors – 6th July 2010 to 1st November 2012 – 28 months. I.e. correspondence in time totalling four years.

In addition to the above I commenced writing my book in May 2013. All being well this will have been published in July 2015 – 25 months. An involvement just in excess of six years.

You will have realised the publication of this book lets the cat officially out of the bag in no uncertain manner. I now await the Pure Leisure Group's reaction. Perhaps they may take a resigned, sagely, philosophical route –"losers handshake – fair play – good on him – cé la vie". On the other hand...! Whatever lies ahead I am prepared for any eventuality. Their rejection of my offer to return the compensation figure could stand me in good stead. In any case what venomous actions could they inflict which would be of any significance in proportion to what has gone before?

Our enforced move from the park indirectly and eventually created a situation where Milnthorpe became our permanent home. Four years later we have found the locals to be both understanding and, as time passed, invigorating. Just the tonic my wife and I needed! Whilst the resultant trauma of the eviction etc. is still in our minds the "Milnthorpe experience" has been of great help in getting us back on an even keel. In fact, I see no reason for ever leaving this proud village, its people and all that it offers.

Statistics given by the park home and holiday caravan magazine in their March 2015 edition reveal the following, and I quote:

"Touring caravans are the most popular leisure accommodation vehicle in the UK, with over half a million in current use. That, alongside 327,000 caravan holiday homes, 174,000 motorhomes and 112,000 residential park homes equals more than one million caravans in total".

Should my book prevent just one family or couple from entering the web of corruption shown therein then "the burning of the midnight oil" will have been more than worthwhile.

Now having entered my 76th year, I take consolation from the thought that my interview for the honour of being granted eternal heavenly life may be successful due to my revelations about evil in this book. I also duly take encouragement from the following 'parable':

A pensioner stood at the pearly gates,
His head was bent and low,
He meekly asked the man of fate
Which way he had to go,
"What have you done?" St. Peter said,
"to seek admission here"
"I lived on a caravan park" said he,
Then whispered in his ear,
To which Saint Peter opened wide the gates,
And beamed on him as well,
"Come right in my friend", he said
"You've had your share of hell"

Printed in Great Britain
by Amazon.co.uk, Ltd.,
Marston Gate.